AF843116

the book of japanese self-care

forest bathing, tea ceremonies, zen meditation, and more

iris law

CICO BOOKS

To Dad, your home-cooked meals nourish my body;
your selfless love nurtures my mind and soul.

Editors: Imogen Valler-Miles and Julia Rink
Designers: Toni Kay and Emily Breen
Commissioning Editor: Kristine Pidkameny
Creative Director: Leslie Harrington
Head of Production: Patricia Harrington
Publisher: Carmel Edmonds

Published in 2026 by CICO Books
An imprint of Ryland Peters & Small Ltd
20–21 Jockey's Fields, London, WC1R 4BW
www.rylandpeters.com
Email: euregulations@rylandpeters.com

10 9 8 7 6 5 4 3 2 1

Text © Iris Law 2026
Design © CICO Books 2026
For photography and illustration credits, see page 143.

ISBN 978-1-80065-672-7

Printed in China

The author's moral rights have been asserted. All rights reserved. No part of this publication may be reproduced, stored in a retrieval system, or transmitted in any form or by any means, electronic, mechanical, photocopying, or otherwise, without the prior permission of the publisher.

A CIP record for this book is available from the British Library.
US Library of Congress CIP data has been applied for.

The authorised representative in the EEA is Authorised Rep Compliance Ltd.,
Ground Floor. 71 Lower Baggot Street,
Dublin, D01 P593, Ireland
www.arccompliance.com

This book does not constitute medical, health, therapeutic, or professional advice, nor is it intended to diagnose, treat, cure, or prevent any disease or medical condition. Readers should not rely on the information in this book as a substitute for professional medical advice, diagnosis, or treatment.

Readers are strongly advised to consult a qualified healthcare professional before engaging in hot spring bathing or related activities, particularly if they are pregnant, elderly, have pre-existing medical conditions, sensitivities to heat or minerals, cardiovascular conditions, skin conditions, or any other health concerns. The author and publisher assume no responsibility or liability for any injury, loss, damage, or adverse effects—direct or indirect—that may result from the use or misuse of the information contained in this book.

MIX
Paper | Supporting responsible forestry
FSC
www.fsc.org
FSC® C008047

contents

introduction

In the summer of 1998, I set foot in Tokyo for the very first time, filled with excitement and curiosity. I had only ever seen it on television and heard friends speak of its fascination—the quality of its food, innovative gadgets, spotless streets, bullet-speed Shinkansen trains, and above all, its well-mannered people and rich cultural heritage. I stayed at a modest hotel in Ueno, in a room so tiny that I couldn't even open my suitcase. That first experience was absolutely eye-opening, marking the beginning of many unforgettable adventures in Japan that would unfold over the next nearly three decades.

Since I lived just a short four-hour flight away from Japan, it became a place I visited more and more often to escape from the noise and busyness in my city, stress at work, and the demands of life.

It was during a winter visit to the rural hot spring town of Noboribetsu in Hokkaido in 2002 that I began to connect with Japan's countryside. That trip ignited a journey of discovery into Japan's rich culture and history. Since then, I have explored many hidden corners of this Land of the Rising Sun and soaked in numerous healing hot springs in some of its most beautiful and secluded locations. These off-the-beaten-path destinations revealed another side of Japan, where cultural traditions have been passed down through generations—it feels almost miraculous that they are still cherished today. Vastly different from the large cities of Tokyo and Osaka, these locales offer a much deeper immersion into Japanese culture and a profound connection to nature.

Japan holds a special place in my heart. Over the years, I've grown to admire the values and philosophies that shape Japanese life. Spending time with locals has blessed me with countless moments of inspiration, not only through conversations, but also through observation. From the joy found in simple, everyday moments to unwavering commitment to upholding a family business legacy, I've witnessed wisdom rooted in acceptance and balance. This way of living encourages embracing life's ups and downs, fostering inner peace and resilience along the way.

Over time, Japan has become not just a place I like to travel to, but a personal healing sanctuary, a place

where I find peace, harmony, and kindness. My curious beginner's mind (see p. 82) is still very much active, as I continue to learn and uncover more with every new visit.

What I love most about Japan is its small, unassuming quality. Nothing feels loud or excessive, everything is considered. Beauty reveals itself in modest gestures and quiet routines. Rather than pursuing impact directly, meaning is built slowly through attention to detail, patience, and respect for ordinary life. These small acts gradually gather depth and create lasting change. The philosophies in this book grow from this way of thinking, reminding us that a fulfilling life is not shaped by constant striving or dramatic achievement, but by caring deeply for what we do, day after day.

When considering health and well-being through the lens of East Asian traditional medicine, the body, mind, and soul cannot be separated. In many Eastern cultures, the idea of "self-care" was rarely spoken of in the past, yet its essence has always been present. Caring for oneself is never only about personal happiness, but a lifelong self-cultivation—a commitment to integrating the body, mind, and soul in ways that positively impact to the family, community, and natural world. When the whole being is at peace, that harmony naturally ripples outward into the lives of others. True holistic well-being stems from balance between self and others, body and spirit, and humanity and nature.

Japanese self-care takes root in Shinto and Buddhism, enriched by Taoist and Confucian teachings. Shinto, Japan's indigenous tradition or often described as the "Japanese religion," emphasizes reverence for nature and purity as expressed through cleansing rituals at shrines. Zen Buddhism teaches simplicity, presence, and an awareness of impermanence that are essential in the practices of *chadō* (the Way of Tea) and *zazen* (Zen meditation). Taoist principles entered Japan alongside traditional Chinese medicine, focusing on dietary guidance, seasonal living, and energy-balancing approaches, while Confucian teachings emphasize harmony in relationships, and that well-being is not attained on an individual level alone but nurtured through family and community bonds.

These traditions offer profound insights, though the full depth extends far beyond the scope of this book, and certainly beyond my own expertise. Still, I believe that some of their key concepts can offer meaningful perspectives that resonate with the spirit of what we will explore together. These concepts are essential to a healthy body, a balanced mind, and a fulfilled soul. Introduced chapter by chapter, they're not meant to be appreciated in isolation. They naturally weave into one another, and in real life are often experienced together within the same moment or practice. To live in the true spirit of these teachings, let them blend and flow across the entire book. Apply them fluidly in daily life to help you see, choose, and care for yourself in both the small, ordinary situations and the bigger decisions in life.

Self-care, to me, is the art of tuning into myself, softly listening to my inner compass, letting my body tell me what I truly need. I reserve time every day to connect my body with the mind and soul, free from noise and distractions. Self-care is not an occasional treat, but a consistent and intentional daily practice. A luxurious spa treatment or a special meal may be a pleasant way to pamper the senses and ease stress once in a while, but these indulgences don't constitute true care for one's being. Authentic self-care requires more proactive and holistic steps that focus on internal health, mental well-being, and spiritual growth through time, rather than offering only surface-level rejuvenation. Self-care is for everyone, it is not a privilege reserved for an elite few.

I invite you to join me on a journey to Japan—into stillness, seasonal harmony, cultural experience, and a way of living that reconnects us with what it means to be fully human. Each chapter includes a self-care ritual—an offering to you to connect with yourself through regular practice. I hope these rituals can support you on your wellness journey, help you live with joy and vitality, and gently guide you to become a more grounded, present version of yourself: the person you are meant to be.

chapter 1

for the body

BEFORE THE MIND CAN QUIET and the soul can open, the body must first be grounded. In Japanese traditions, the body is not simply a physical dwelling, it is our sacred temple. Whether through the warmth of *onsen* waters or the nourishment of mindful everyday cooking, care for the body invites us back into our sensation, rhythm, and presence.

Japanese culture teaches that well-being begins with consistent daily rituals that embrace simplicity and harmony with nature. They serve as reminders that the body finds balance and ease through modest, human, and unhurried practices.

This chapter is an invitation to reacquaint yourself with your body, and to rediscover the truth that caring for the body is the foundation upon which all deeper forms of self-care are built.

温泉

onsen (hot spring)

Located in the northwestern segment of the Pacific "Ring of Fire," Japan has an unusually dense network of volcanoes, mountains, magma, and underground water pathways. Over millions of years, this has created one of the world's richest concentrations of hot springs, known in Japanese as *onsen*.

a gift of nature

Japan is blessed with plentiful rain and snow that supply the abundant underground water system. The water makes its way from the mountains into the ground, seeping through cracks of rocks, soil, and sediment. Heated by hot rocks and the Earth's magma chambers, it dissolves and picks up minerals along the way. This process can take up to 50–100 years, during which time the water becomes a concentrated mineral solution that emerges on the surface as a hot spring.

These naturally heated, mineral-rich waters are believed to heal ailments and support health and well-being. Through the ages, emperors, soldiers, and villagers have sought rest, rejuvenation, and healing from the therapeutic waters, and many hot spring towns in Japan feature legends of animals discovering the springs' healing powers, along with shrines honoring deities of medicine and recovery.

Nowadays, hot spring facilities are established nationwide, each one featuring its own story and heritage,

"Onsen *has become my sanctuary; a place to rest, heal, and restore my energy."*

celebrating Japanese excellence in hospitality and boasting different spring waters for relaxation or to treat certain health conditions. Over two decades of traveling across Japan, I have discovered more than 100 secluded hot springs tucked away in mountains, valleys, and along remote coastlines.

Onsen has become my sanctuary; a place to rest, heal, and restore my energy. Falling in love with *onsen* has been life-changing for me. Soaking in a bath is time dedicated fully to myself—a time to destress, to declutter my mind, to be still, to self-reflect, to tune in to my body. Inside an *onsen*, the gentle heat begins to unfasten the body's defences: muscles loosen, breath deepens, tension gradually slips away. In the quiet steamy space, I pay closer attention to sensations that are usually numbed by the busyness of daily life. An *onsen* experience is far more than a bath—to me, it is a spiritual, awe-inspiring, and transformative encounter with the healing power and timeless beauty of Mother Nature.

born of springs, shaped by water

Japan is a nation whose story begins in water. As an island shaped and surrounded by the sea with abundant rain, rivers, and hot springs, water is a living presence that cleanses, connects, and carries blessings. It has always been the force binding Japan's traditions to its identity, long treated as a companion to daily life—the Japanese people live beside it, pray with it, and entrust their tired bodies to it.

Spiritually, rivers wash away the dust of the otherworld, and people are symbolically reborn through purification rituals with water. In daily life, rain, snowmelt, and hot springs are felt to be part of a cycle: the sky offers water, the mountains hold it, the earth warms and mineralizes it, and eventually it oozes up again as a steaming pool where people soothe their bodies.

In Japanese traditions of bathing and purification, cleansing has always extended beyond the physical body. Shinto practices of purification recognize that impurity clings not only to the skin, but also to the more subtle layers of our being. At the *torii* gate of a Shinto shrine, worshippers purify themselves by rinsing their hands and mouth before stepping into the sacred grounds to the *kami* spirits. In another more intense form of purification, pilgrims stand beneath waterfalls as a prayer for renewal and rebirth by the powerful flow of the cascade.

In Buddhist teachings, bathing and washing are believed to remove worldly defilement and help dispel illness and suffering. Water also symbolizes the

fluid, ever-changing nature of existence, that all things have a continual cycle of renewal. At the same time, it embodies compassion and generosity, nourishing every form of life.

Hot springs in Japan connect the people, land, and religion. They bridge the boundaries between self and world, body and spirit. Entering a thermal spring echoes a religious purification ritual: each bathing experience begins with washing off dirt outside the tub, and only then does the cleansed naked body enter the shared water. The warm embrace of the spring can soften the body enough to release what it has been carrying.

bathing culture

Japan has a long-standing and distinctive bathing culture that is exceptionally well-preserved. Japanese *onsen* and bathing practices have played a significant role in shaping the country's history and culture. What sets Japan apart from the rest of the world is how deeply bathing is woven into everyday life, etiquette, religion, architecture, and the country's identity, and how it has been practiced from ancient times and very much into the present.

Communal bathing is a cherished ritual, an everyday habit, and a social activity that takes place in a neighborhood *sento* (public baths), at *onsen ryokan* (inns with hot spring baths), or at a temple as a purification ritual. It serves as a time to rejuvenate and recharge oneself after each day's busyness and hard work, to connect with the community, or simply to be still to reset the body and mind.

People bathe together to relax, talk, and feel part of a community. In these shared spaces, bathing naked carries a cultural meaning: it represents shedding social status and barriers, allowing people to return to an original unmasked state where everyone can meet openly and authentically. This openness and togetherness are what make *onsen* bathing culture so unique and important in Japan.

Longevity is closely linked to strong social bonds. Japanese culture honors community connection where people come together with a shared purpose. This cultivates a sense of belonging that is valued as much as diet and exercise in extending both lifespan and healthspan. In Okinawa Prefecture, people live well into their nineties and this region has one of the highest numbers of centenarians in the world. Japanese people value participating in communal activities and believe that strong support from others is essential for living a long, healthy life.

Having a strong social support system is like having our own team cheering us on. When we know there are people we can lean on, everyday stress feels a little lighter. It supports our physical health, too, lowering the risk of chronic illnesses and helping us bounce back faster when we are unwell. And on tough days, having someone who listens or checks in can make a huge difference in how we cope. People with a solid support system tend to handle challenges better, recover more quickly, and simply feel happier and more fulfilled.

onsen type	alleged benefits
simple	*low mineral content, gentle on skin, suitable for all ages*
chloride	*retains body heat, improves circulation, good for cold sensitivity*
bicarbonate	*smooths skin, mildly exfoliating, often called "beauty baths"*
sulfate	*supports joint health, circulation, and recovery from fatigue*
carbon dioxide	*fizzy sensation, improves blood flow, lowers blood pressure*
iron	*reddish water, deeply warming, helps with anemia and fatigue*
acidic	*antibacterial, effective for skin ailments, cleansing properties*
iodine	*boosts immunity, warms body, supports thyroid health*
sulfur	*distinct smell, good for skin conditions and joint pain*
radium	*mildly radioactive, boosts metabolism, believed to aid immunity*

the healing waters

Japan classifies *onsen* into 10 main types of mineral springs, with water typically maintained at 100–108°F (38–42°C). Each type has its own mineral composition and associated alleged health effects (see table above).

Hot springs in volcanic regions are often sulfur-rich and acidic, while non-volcanic areas tend to yield carbonate, chloride, or iodine-rich alkaline waters. Depending on the local geology, a spring can also be a natural blend of several water types.

Some springs are considered to be medicinal and have attracted hot-spring pilgrims and enthusiasts seeking relief from ailments for over a thousand years. These waters contain higher concentrations of minerals and gases that are believed to offer specific therapeutic benefits. Medical doctors and researchers at Japan's hot-spring institutes have carried out studies on how these *onsen* waters affect the body. For many Japanese people, *onsen* bathing is a holistic form of care; beyond recreation and relaxation, it's also a way to receive healing and "medicine" gifted by nature.

Our skin is the largest organ of the human body. When soaking in an *onsen*, the warm water dilates blood vessels, increases circulation, and allows minerals such as calcium, sodium, magnesium, and potassium to penetrate through the skin's outer layers. Through a process called transdermal absorption, trace elements can enter the body to potentially support metabolism, ease muscle tension, and aid recovery. At the same time, heat opens pores and relaxes connective tissue. Immersion in warm water also activates the parasympathetic nervous system, which shifts the body from stress mode into a state of rest and relaxation. The result is a gentle, whole-body therapy in which skin, muscles, and nervous system all potentially benefit from the minerals rising in earth's geothermal springs.

toji—the hot spring therapy

Literally meaning "hot water cure," *toji* is a traditional therapeutic hot spring bathing method in Japan that has been practiced since the Nara period (710–784 CE). It usually takes place in *onsen* inns (photos pp. 19–21) where people stay for days or weeks, bathing in healing springs multiple times a day to support health and recovery. Wounded warriors once bathed and rested in medicinal *onsen* to heal physical and mental injuries from battle, while farmers used *toji* during the fall and winter after the year's harvest to recover from pain and exhaustion after hard physical work. Today, it is considered a form of preventive care to rejuvenate the body and help alleviate certain health conditions, often offered as a wellness program at modest *toji* lodgings, where the focus is on slowing down, resting, soaking repeatedly in healing waters, and eating simple, nutritious meals to support the body's own healing capacity.

There are several famous *toji* hot spring towns in Japan. I had the opportunity to experience a comprehensive *toji* program in the bubbling hot spring town of Beppu (opposite)—also known as the "City of Steam" for its abundant geothermal activity. Upon arriving at the *toji* lodge Nanoka Hitomeguri, I first completed a health questionnaire to assess my current physical condition and lifestyle. This was followed by a consultation

with an on-site nurse and hot spring specialist, who evaluated cardiovascular function, inflammation, chronic pain, and stress levels.

Based on the results, I received recommendations for the type of hot spring most suitable for my condition, along with guidelines on how many times to soak per day, ideal water temperature, bathing duration, and rest intervals. The program also included cooking lessons using local ingredients and fermented foods, a lecture on gut health, and a miso-making session. Before departure, there was a final health check to compare post-*toji* results with the initial evaluation.

Nanoka Hitomeguri is a *toji* initiative created by Shizuka Kanno, who grew up in Beppu. She explains, "For the human mind and body to heal, I believe it is essential to once again feel the flow of time in harmony with nature. *Toji* is the perfect place to let go of excess and reexamine yourself. The best part of *toji* is believing in and nurturing the natural healing powers of your body and mind by strengthening your immune system." Kanno continues to devote herself to *toji* research and to sharing *toji* culture with people both within and beyond Japan.

onsen etiquette and precautions

While *onsen* bathing is deeply restorative, it is important to observe certain etiquette and precautions so that the experience remains safe and beneficial.

♦ Wash thoroughly before entering the bath area—cleanse your body at the shower stations.

♦ Hydrate well—drink water before and after bathing.

♦ Avoid prolonged bathing or water that is too hot—this may cause dizziness, dehydration, or fainting, and the high temperatures can place extra strain on the heart and circulatory system. Each session is best kept to around 10–15 minutes.

♦ Listen to your body—step out if you feel dizzy, weak, or overheated.

♦ Respect etiquette—keep towels and hair out of the water, maintain quiet conversation, and be considerate of others.

♦ Cool down gradually—rest outside the bath between soaks.

♦ Avoid drinking alcohol before bathing; it increases the risk of fainting, overheating, or accidents.

♦ Refrain from using the bath if you have open wounds or contagious conditions.

♦ Ease your body slowly into the hot water to avoid sudden shock to the system.

♦ Consult a doctor beforehand if you have cardiovascular conditions, high blood pressure, or are pregnant.

♦ Don't drink the water unless you are sure it is safe to do so. Most *onsen* waters are intended for bathing and only some are officially approved for drinking (*insen* in Japanese)—even then, only small amounts should be consumed when fresh and taken directly from the source.

home *toji* self-care ritual

Not everyone has easy access to *onsen*, but you can create a soothing *toji*-inspired bath at home as a simple ritual to support health and vitality. In many Japanese households, there is an *ofuro* (deep seated soaking bathtub) where a relaxing soak can be enjoyed at the end of the day.

- Fill the bathtub with warm water (not too hot—around 99–102°F (37–39°C) is ideal).
- Add about 2 cups (500 g) of Epsom salt or magnesium flakes to the water; these can help soothe sore muscles and ease tension.
- Dilute 5 to 20 drops of pure essential oil of your choice with 1 tablespoon of carrier oil. Then add this oil blend to the bath salt so it disperses more evenly and does not irritate the skin. A blend of lavender, geranium, and ylang-ylang creates a deeply relaxing bath, or you may choose Japanese scents such as *hinoki* (Japanese cypress), *hiba* (another type of Japanese cypress), or yuzu (Japanese citron).
- Dim the bathroom lights, or light a candle to soften the atmosphere.
- Slowly immerse your body in the warm bath, giving yourself time to adjust to the temperature.
- Take a few deep breaths. Inhale warmth and ease; exhale worries, stress, and any heavy thoughts.
- Allow your breathing to settle into a natural rhythm, and soak for about 15–20 minutes.
- Gently notice sensations in your body as you bathe. Invite your body and mind to relax in the quiet space.
- Before finishing, take three deeper breaths and offer a simple moment of gratitude to the healing water.
- Step out of the bath, acknowledging this as a small transformation. Notice the lightness in your limbs and the easier breath—signs that your body has released something it no longer needs.
- Drink a glass or two of water to rehydrate, or prepare a cup of herbal tea to carry this calmness with you into sleep.

料理

ryori (cuisine)

There are many good reasons why Japanese *ryori*, or cuisine, has captured the global spotlight. Every meal is a promise of flavor, elegance, and artistry crafted from fresh, seasonal, local ingredients. Japanese *ryori* is not simply food preparation and cooking. It is an exhibition of culinary tradition, seasonality, health, and spirituality.

the heart of Japanese *ryori*

Visitors flock to Japan for fine sushi *omakase* (chef's selection) in Tokyo that requires prepaid advance reservation, and exquisite *kaiseki* dining in Kyoto featuring artistically prepared courses, while modern favorites like *ramen* (soup noodles), *yakitori* (grilled chicken skewers), and *okonomiyaki* (Japanese pancakes) are enjoyed in bustling casual eateries with long waiting queues.

To many foreigners, these iconic dishes represent the essence of Japan. Yet beyond these celebrated styles, Japanese *ryori* is much more than indulgence or presentation. It is living in harmony with the seasons, embracing humble ingredients, and transforming simplicity into nourishment for the body and soul.

Every style of cuisine in Japan reflects harmony and balance between flavors, textures, and the natural rhythm of life, served with meticulous attention to aesthetics. Simple ingredients become local fare that reflects family heritage, regional identity, patience, and love—a harmonious expression connecting people, land, and sea.

Essential to Japanese cuisine is the principle of *shun*—aligning meals with the season. Eating seasonally is a way of life, connecting families to the land and its cycles. Nowadays, when ingredients are available year-round, we have forgotten that humans evolved by consuming foods only when they were naturally present. Over thousands of years, our bodies have adapted to seasonal patterns; the nutrients we need shift according to the time of the year. Foods are more nutrient-dense when they flourish under the conditions of the seasons they are meant to grow in, while eating out-of-season produce can disrupt our internal circannual rhythm. When we align our diet with nature's calendar, we support the body's functions and overall well-being. It is also a way of honoring the body, our sacred temple, letting it move joyfully with the rhythm of nature.

We turn away from the grandeur of *omakase* counters and *kaiseki* fine dining to step into the kitchens of Japan's homes and villages. The heart of Japanese food culture is *washoku*, traditional Japanese food that nourishes families every day and embodies the wisdom of ancestors. *Wa* means harmony and *shoku* means food—Japanese cuisine is a meal of harmony. A family menu is simple: one soup and three dishes—*ichiju sansai*. There is usually a grilled, a simmered, and a raw dish, served with rice, soup, and pickles (above, p. 26). *Washoku* is a daily act of self-care rather than an occasional treat.

Before beginning a meal, family members say *itadakimasu*—literally "I humbly receive." This simple phrase expresses thanks not only to the person who prepared the food, but also to the farmers, producers, and everyone involved in bringing it to the table. Gratitude is also extended to the rain, sunlight, and soil that nurtured the ingredients. *Itadakimasu* is a cultural ritual that honors the interconnectedness of human and nature.

umami—the fifth taste of harmony

Beyond the familiar sweet, salty, sour, and bitter, Japanese cooking centers the fifth taste—*umami*. Difficult to articulate, it is an unspoken depth of flavor that lingers on the tongue and settles gently in the body—savory, rounded, deeply satisfying. In Japan, it has long been recognized as the taste that brings a meal into emotional balance.

Umami plays an essential role in Japanese *ryori* culture, both as a flavor and as a culinary philosophy. It is subtle, complex, experiential, and only becomes noticeable when combined with other flavors and aromas. For example, it is found in a piece of *kombu* (kelp) (top right) simmered in water, the savory sweetness released from *shiitake* mushrooms (bottom right), and the richness of miso or soy sauce (p. 34) developed through fermentation and aging. *Ryori* values balance and clarity, enhancing flavor without overpowering the ingredients' original taste.

Umami is soulful—a taste of comfort, a taste of home, a taste that restores the body. It brings harmony, soothes the heart, and calms the senses. A warm bowl of miso soup (p. 30) or a sip of clear *dashi* broth invites slowness and mindfulness, something that cannot be savored in a rush.

a living legacy of fermentation

Fermentation has existed for thousands of years in many cultures, yet global interest in fermented food was only renewed in the last decade. After World War II, people gradually turned away from traditional culinary practices. Urbanization changed lifestyles significantly, work hours increased, and demand grew for ready-to-eat food requiring minimal preparation.

The world shifted to industrial food systems, and ultra-processed food products—which are high in sugar and unhealthy fats and low in fiber and essential nutrients—have substituted our diets. This dietary change is closely linked to poorer gut health as the microbiome and intestinal barrier are disrupted, leading to inflammation and increasing the risk of chronic diseases.

Fermented foods are packed with probiotics and compounds that support a healthy gut microbiome. Studies highlight their role in digestion, immunity, and mental health through the gut-brain axis—the two-way communication between the digestive and nervous systems. After the COVID-19 pandemic, awareness of gut health intensified as evidence suggests that a compromised microbiome is associated with more serious symptoms and increased anxiety and depression.

In Japan, fermentation is a cultural cornerstone that has shaped the culinary scene for over two millennia. It is a subtle alchemy—a partnership between human hands, raw ingredients, and the unseen work of microorganisms. In a culture where meals are small rituals of gratitude, fermented foods are everyday reminders that transformation works its magic slowly and quietly.

Koji, also known as "Japan's national fungus," is a delicate mold cultivated on rice, barley, or soybeans. It is essential to the making of Japan's iconic seasonings and beverages. Acting as a natural catalyst, *koji* breaks down proteins and starches into amino acids and natural sweetness, creating the foundation of *umami*.

Traditional *washoku* boasts an abundance of fermented food. Some of Japan's core fermented foods and seasonings are:

Miso: A blend of soybeans, salt, and *koji*, aged for months or years; a staple in Japanese kitchens.

***Shoyu* (soy sauce):** A dark, savory liquid seasoning made through months to years of fermentation of soybeans, wheat, rice, salt, and *koji*.

***Natto*:** Fermented soybeans with a distinctive aroma and sticky texture; high in probiotics, protein, potassium, and vitamin K2.

***Nihonshu* (Japanese rice wine, more commonly called *sake*):** Brewed from rice and *koji*; used both in cooking and as a beverage.

***Tsukemono* (pickled vegetables):** Seasonal vegetables fermented in salt, rice bran, or *koji*; often served as palate cleansers or side dishes (right).

A living example of Japan's fermentation heritage is found in Yuzawa in Akita Prefecture, a region of heavy snowfall and harsh winters where strong fermentation traditions help people endure the long, cold months. Founded in 1867, Yamamo Miso and Soy Sauce Brewery has preserved this craft for over 150 years, passed through seven generations to the current owner, Yasushi Takahashi.

Yamamo takes pride in its art of fermentation. The brewery continues to make miso and *shoyu* (opposite) by hand—using pure water, soybeans, and Akita-grown rice—aging them in wooden barrels. The process involves careful control in timing, temperature, and microbial balance, carried out slowly and patiently by highly skilled artisans who have honed their techniques over many years to craft products of exceptional quality.

During my visit, I joined a tasting tour followed by lunch at the brewery's Japanese-fusion styled restaurant, Astronomica. I was led through the brewery, moving from one section to another, each one filled with the rich fragrance of fermenting mash, which is composed of soybeans, koji, and salt. Along the way, I was introduced to the history of Yamamo and the making of its products. I stopped at several stations inside the brewery to taste miso and *shoyu* of different ages before sitting down to dishes prepared with Yamamo's in-house Viamver® yeast.

Sampling miso across its aging spectrum reveals an evolving depth and character. The flavor of the one-year miso still carried a gentle sweetness but had deepened into a mellow roundness; the five-year miso had darkened and thickened, with notes of cocoa, dried fruit, aged wood, and touches of molasses; and finally, the 30-year miso felt divine—its glossy surface and resin-like texture held smoky, deep *umami* complexity. The experience left me in awe of how invisible microbes shape character, and how bacteria on human hands collaborate with natural ingredients to produce such a high quality of miso.

Honoring fermentation heritage teaches that transformation takes time. Character is shaped by patience; healing is quiet work that cannot be rushed; our well-being is restored through steady, gentle, and attentive care each and every day.

mountain cuisine—gourmet of nature's bounty

Japan is a land of mountains; more than 70 percent of its terrain is covered in forest. In harsh, cold environments, food was once a necessity for survival rather than pleasure. People relied on what the wildness provided: foraging *sansai* (wild mountain vegetables), catching *ayu* river fish, preserving vegetables and meat to sustain snowy winter, growing *soba* buckwheat where rice could not grow. Over time, this humble mountain cooking matured into a unique regional culture. The wildest of plants, which once served the ancestors because there was nothing else to eat, have become treasured local specialties.

One of the most enchanting places to experience this tradition is the secluded Iya Valley, located in Tokushima Prefecture on Shikoku Island. Ochiai Village, a historic settlement recognized for its cultural value, feels like a step back in time. Legends and folklore say fallen warriors of the late twelfth century first settled here, and even today, it remains quite untouched. Villagers live in traditional thatched-roof houses amid a mystical landscape, often blanketed by drifting clouds—a scene that always leaves me in awe of nature's splendor.

One late fall, I visited the Ochiai Village (opposite) and stayed at one of the farmhouses of Tougenkyo-Iya—a village revitalization project run by American Japanologist Alex Kerr. During my stay, I spent a day with a local family from whom I learned to make *soba*

noodles from scratch, using 100 percent buckwheat flour, stone-milled from Iya-grown grains that give the noodles a distinctively coarse texture. Afternoon was spent wandering through hillside fields and listening to tales of life in these secluded valleys. As evening fell, the grandmother arrived with a basket of freshly picked wild vegetables, potatoes, tofu, wild boar, and homemade miso paste for making a hearty *nabe* (hotpot). The food was simple yet wholesome and full of flavor. Cooking alongside the family wasn't just about food—it was sharing the traditions that they take pride in with an outsider, with laughter and joy. Their hospitality made me feel like family—a beautiful exchange of cultures and languages.

On another occasion in Niigata Prefecture, Japan's "snow country," I had a one-of-a-kind dining experience during my stay at a boutique hotel, Satoyama Jujo. Here, Michelin-starred chef Keiko Kuwakino—head chef of the hotel's restaurant, Sanaburi, and ranked among Japan's top 100 chefs—serves plant-forward, mountain-to-table cuisine that has earned global recognition and numerous awards. Our conversation revealed her cooking philosophy of living in harmony with nature. After moving to Niigata 11 years ago, she spent most days of the week in the mountains, observing the life cycle of plants and learning foraging and fermentation practices from elders. Her cuisine tells the story of the land, sustainability, and the deep connection between people and nature. For her, cooking is never just about filling the stomach, it is nourishment for *kokoro*—the heart-mind—carrying love, care, connection, and a quiet hope for well-being.

Chef Keiko's foraging practice opened a new world of flavor. She marvels at the richness of wild ingredients in the mountains and the array of flavors. These hand-gathered treasures represent true luxury in her eyes—something rare, tied to a specific place and season, and impossible to buy. "Through foraging, I learned humility, patience, and the deeper beauty that lies beyond gastronomy: the wisdom of nature and its connection to human health and life," she shared. In traditional Japanese cooking, she embraces *mottainai*—the concept of no waste, using all parts of the plant as much as possible. In a world where ingredients like wagyu and caviar can dominate the scene of luxury dining, chef Keiko finds greater purpose in creating extraordinary flavors from the simplest ingredients, and carrying forward the wisdom of snow country traditions through practicing "fermentation for living," as she called it—a vision shared by both Sanaburi and Satoyama Jujo in their quest to redefine luxury.

Both experiences in Iya and Niigata were celebrations of local abundance. What touched me most was how nourishing these experiences felt. Mindful cooking of the fresh, seasonal foods gave me a sense of well-being. I was reminded that health is not only about nutrients but about gratitude for the land, the seasons, and the people who cultivate them. Mountain cuisine is an immersion into rural Japan's soul, where everything gently aligns with nature's calendar—an absolute nourishment for both body and spirit.

shojin ryori—the spiritual flavors

Buddhism was introduced to Japan in the sixth century, and its principles of non-killing and dietary discipline laid the foundation of *shojin ryori*—Buddhist temple cuisine. Later, in the thirteenth-century Kamakura period, with the rise of Zen Buddhism and the influence of Zen monk Dōgen Zenji, the structure and cooking methods became more formalized. *Shojin* means "earnest devotion to practice"—its cuisine puts emphasis on ingredients, meal planning, and preparation that support the monks' spiritual discipline and long periods of meditation training. It is a plant-based meal course, free of meat, fish, and pungent flavors. Chefs embody centuries of Zen tradition guided by Dōgen's teachings of the Three Minds:

- The joyful mind to cook and serve with joy.
- The nurturing mind to care for food and guests with warmth and kindness.
- The great mind to carry a purposeful, generous, and impartial attitude.

During my visit to Dewa Sanzan in Yamagata Prefecture, I visited Saikan—a temple lodge on Mount Haguro—for a traditional Buddhist vegetarian meal. Dewa Sanzan refers to the three holy mountains of Dewa—Haguro, Gassan, and Yudono. For over 1,400 years, these ancient peaks have been a center of *Shugendo*, a syncretic faith blending Shinto, Buddhism, and mountain worship. Pilgrims have long journeyed here to seek rebirth and enlightenment through rigorous spiritual training. Haguro symbolizes the present life, while Gassan represents the past, and Yudono the future, forming a sacred triad that reflects the cycle of existence.

To follow the footsteps of pilgrims, I hiked up Mount Haguro to reach the summit where Saikan is located. The trail consists of 2,446 stone steps winding through a serene forest of towering ancient *sugi* cedar trees (below). Along the way, I passed a stunning five-story wooden pagoda

(p. 39 left) rebuilt in the fourteenth century, and a thousand-year-old grandpa cedar tree, famously known as *Jiji-sugi* (p. 39 right), with a massive trunk encircled by a *shimenawa* sacred rope and believed to house a dwelling spirit, or *kami*. The atmosphere was deeply spiritual and mystical, reflecting nature's divine essence in Japanese mountain worship traditions.

After a steady climb, I reached Saikan. Here, pilgrims and visitors alike can experience Mount Haguro-style *shojin ryori* passed down since ancient times. A tray with multiple small dishes was brought to my table, featuring fried and pickled *sansai*, tofu, and wild herbs. Depending on the season, wild vegetables like *takenoko* (bamboo shoots), *honseri* (wild parsley), *fukinoto* (butterbur buds), and *kogomi* (a kind of edible fern) can be harvested in Mount Haguro. The portion was modest, honoring the concept of *mottainai*—a gentle reminder to avoid waste. I enjoyed the lightly seasoned dishes, allowing me to savor the distinct flavors of the mountain ingredients—a refreshing bitterness and slight astringency, balanced with sweetness and earthy undertones. These dishes reflect the simplicity and ascetic practices of pilgrims who had visited these mountains in the past. Ending this pilgrimage-like hike at sacred Dewa Sanzan with *shojin ryori* felt like a blessing; I left feeling nourished and cleansed by the spiritual flavors.

ryori as everyday self-care

You can prepare Japanese *ryori* at home using simple ingredients that warm your heart and soul. Incorporating fermented foods and seasonings into daily cooking not only adds *umami* to your dishes and keeps your gut healthy, but is also an active participation in the process of transformative inner growth.

DASHI BROTH

The foundation of Japanese cooking, dashi *is light, clear, deeply savory, and ready in minutes. It's the essence of umami—simple and delightful.*

1–1½ oz. (30–40 g) *niboshi* (dried anchovies or sardines; leave out for vegetarian version)
4-inch (1 x 10-cm) piece of *kombu* (dried kelp)

MAKES 1 LITER/QUART

Remove the heads and guts of the *niboshi* with a knife or scissors to prevent a bitter taste.

Place the *niboshi* and *kombu* in a pot with 1 quart/liter of water. Leave to soak for at least 30 minutes, or overnight for a deeper flavor.

Place the pot over a medium heat. Just before the water boils, remove the *kombu* to avoid a slimy texture. Simmer the water over a low heat for another 6–8 minutes.

Skim off any scum or foam that rises to the surface.

Turn off the heat and let it steep for another 2–5 minutes to allow the *umami* to infuse.

Remove the *niboshi* using a sieve/strainer, and discard.

The *dashi* is now ready to use in miso soup, or as a soup base for *udon, soba,* and *nabe.*

Store in the fridge for 3–4 days, or in the freezer for up to 3 months.

NABE HOTPOT

Making a hearty hotpot at home is truly soul-warming. You can use any vegetables of your choice, but it is best to use seasonal vegetables, adding meat if desired. Nabe *is quick and easy to make, high in protein and fiber, and deeply satisfying, especially during cold winter nights. It's best to cook it in a clay ceramic pot as this will help to draw out the flavors of the ingredients.*

3⅓ cups (800 ml) *dashi*
½ *gobo* (burdock root), cut into pieces
5 large Japanese cabbage leaves, cut into pieces
½ (2–2.5 oz./50–70 g) leek, cut into slices
7 oz. (200 g) *daikon* radish, cut into pieces
3½ oz. (100 g) fresh *maitake* or *shiitake* mushrooms
1 pack (12 oz./350 g) of tofu, cut into pieces
4 tbsp miso (any type is fine)
7 oz. (200 g) pork or beef, thinly sliced (optional)

SERVES 2

In a ceramic pot, bring the *dashi* to the boil, add the *gobo, daikon,* cabbage, and leek, then simmer for about 5 minutes.

Add the mushrooms and tofu and simmer for another 3 minutes.

Add the miso and stir well.

Add the sliced meat (if using), bring to the boil, then switch off the heat. It's ready to serve.

chapter 2

for the mind

ONCE THE BODY HAS SOFTENED AND SETTLED, the mind becomes a gentler place to enter. Japanese traditions do not seek to conquer or control the mind, but to find harmony with it. Calmness is not forced, it arises naturally through rhythm and presence. Practices of forest bathing, the Way of Tea, and seated meditation guide us into stillness, where thoughts can be observed, where awareness expands.

The Japanese understanding of "mind" is not confined to thought alone. It lives in the same space as feeling, intuition, and emotions. All of these are held within the concept of *kokoro*, a word that means both "mind" and "heart" together. This chapter invites you to connect with your inner landscape—*kokoro*—the living center where clarity, calm, and compassion originate.

森林浴

shinrin-yoku (forest bathing)

Originating in Japan, *shinrin-yoku* literally means "forest bathing." It is not taking a bath in the forest, nor is it a hike, or simply a relaxation; it is a multisensory nature immersion experience and a research- and evidence-based practice. It's not a treatment for illness, but a form of preventive medicine and ecotherapy that can bring positive health benefits to improve our well-being.

where nature and humanity breathe as one

In Japan, people and nature have always blended softly and seamlessly together. Rather than something to conquer or escape to, nature is a companion, mentor, and spiritual leader. "Nature is not separate from mankind in Japanese culture," explains Dr. Qing Li, a world-leading scientist in forest medicine based in Japan. The forest heals because humans were never meant to separate from it.

As more people leave rural areas to pursue work in cities, the innate connection humans once had with nature has been eroded. With rising stress-related illnesses as a result of rapid technological growth and urbanization, *shinrin-yoku* was introduced in 1982 by the Japanese government as an initiative intended to support citizens' well-being. Researchers began measuring its physiological effects, identifying significant benefits in stress reduction and improved immunity and

mental well-being. In 2006, Akasawa Forest in Nagano was designated the first certified Forest Therapy Base in Japan, and now there are about 60 certified forests across the country. *Shinrin-yoku* later gained global attention, gradually becoming a widely recognized approach to enhancing holistic health. Certification programs outside Japan also began to be established to standardize training for forest bathing guides.

Although *shinrin-yoku* did not originate from any religious tradition, it resonates with Shinto and Zen traditions that emphasize harmony and connection between humans and nature. In Shinto belief, forests are sacred dwellings of *kami*, or divine spirits, and entering into the forest is an act of reverence and communion with the natural world. Likewise, Zen teaches mindfulness and impermanence —stillness, presence, and living in harmony with nature have been practiced for centuries. In this way, *shinrin-yoku* also reflects *shizen*, the Japanese sense of moving in quiet, unforced harmony with the natural world. These parallels explain the practice's seamless compatibility with Japan's nature-oriented sensibilities.

why we need nature now more than ever

From the moment the alarm goes off in the morning, the mind starts running. Before even getting out of bed, thoughts rush in, there are messages to check. The day begins in a hurry, the commute is spent navigating traffic or squeezing into crowded subways, mentally running through the day's to-do list and imagined scenarios to anticipate what else might come up. At work, the mind splinters across meetings scheduled one after another, juggling tasks that never pause. After work, there are errands to run, social commitments, family care, or unfinished work waiting. By evening, the body feels tired, but the mind refuses to settle, winding down by scrolling devices or watching television until sleep takes over—only for the cycle to repeat the next morning. For many of us, this rhythm has become the default.

Modern life pulls the mind into endless analysis, screens, and multitasking to optimize every moment. Productivity and efficiency become obsessions. Every day is packed with actions, information, and noise. We trust facts but not intuition; chase outcomes rather than letting things unfold in their own rhythm. The world has turned more digital day by day; using a phone or computer to perform our daily tasks almost seems like an imperative rather than a choice.

Many are addicted to screens; Dr. Qing Li calls this unhealthy behavior of overusing technology "technostress." Our brain is relentlessly overstimulated, while our senses and feelings grow numb and quiet. These modern stressors are intense—our body's stress hormones remain elevated around the clock, causing chronic inflammation. If we allow this kind of lifestyle to continue, it can disrupt the body's pathways, damage the organs, and weaken the brain's circuits, raising the risk of physical and mental disorders.

We have forgotton that nature played a big part in how our ancestors lived and evolved. This was a time when the digital background didn't exist, when there was no economic performance to measure. Our ancestors followed the flow of the seasons and respected the flow of life.

Our body clock, or circadian rhythm, directs the organs' functions and processes according to the daylight cycle. Taking a walk in the forest makes us feel good because it is in our DNA to have a desire for nature. There is something gentle and delightful, yet mysterious and powerful about nature—it is never in a rush. In an age where stress has become a modern epidemic, finding stillness in an overstimulated

world is vital, and Mother Nature offers one of the most powerful remedies.

how the forest heals—the science behind *shinrin-yoku*

A mindful connection with nature can make a big difference to our overstimulated brain and body. According to Amos Clifford, founder of the Association of Nature and Forest Therapy Guides and Programs, a US-based organization that trains and certifies forest bathing guides globally, "Forest bathing offers an antidote to our stress-filled and nature-starved lives with a gentle, mindful approach to being with nature."

What sets Japanese *shinrin-yoku* apart from forest bathing practices elsewhere is the depth of scientific research on the topic, evidencing how time in nature could actually make us happier and healthier. Dr. Qing Li and Dr. Yoshifumi Miyazaki in Japan have done extensive research in forest bathing, which has demonstrated its positive impact on physiological well-being, such as lowering blood pressure, boosting immunity, reducing stress, and improving mood and focus. Forest bathing takes a whole person approach and recognizes the intrinsic healing capacity within each individual.

Forest environments are rich in biodiversity, soil microbes, negative ions, and protective organic compounds emitted by trees. These elements make green settings much richer in phytoncides (antimicrobial compounds) than blue settings such as lakes or oceans. Released by trees and especially abundant in conifers, phytoncides give forests their distinctive scents. They are the trees' own natural medicine against insects, bacteria, and fungi, and it turns out that we, too, can benefit from inhaling these forest-scented chemicals during forest bathing. The body responds by increasing the production of natural killer (NK) cells—our immune system's frontline defenders that have the ability to destroy harmful or abnormal cells. This heightened protection can last for weeks after a time spent with trees.

Modern neuroscience helps us understand how the brain responds to being in nature. When we enter natural environments, activity in the amygdala (the brain's danger detection center) decreases, while the parasympathetic nervous system (the body's calming system) becomes more active. Our brain communicates with the body in two main ways—through the nervous system, networks of neurons use neurotransmitters to regulate functions and guide movement, emotion, and cognition; while hormones travel through the bloodstream to regulate processes such as metabolism, stress response, and energy balance. Together, these messengers form a continuous dialogue between the brain and the body, softening the body's alarms with each breath of forest air.

The table below lists some of the neurotransmitters and hormones that shape how we feel and think. They work together cohesively rather than independently.

When we practice forest bathing, our mindful presence in among the trees lifts serotonin. The gentle sound and scents of the environment offer a

neurotransmitters/ hormones	key functions
serotonin	*supports mood stability, emotional balance, and a sense of well-being; also influences sleep and appetite*
dopamine	*drives motivation, reward, pleasure, and focus; plays a major role in attention and decision-making*
GABA (gamma-aminobutyric acid)	*the brain's calming messenger that reduces anxiety, quiets overactivity, and promotes relaxation*
oxytocin	*often called the "love hormone," promotes social bonding, trust, and reduces stress*
cortisol	*the primary stress hormone; important for energy regulation and alertness, but can impact mood and cognition when chronically high*
adrenaline	*triggers the fight-or-flight response, heightening focus and physical readiness in stressful moments*
endorphines	*natural pain-relieving hormones that boost mood and create feelings of comfort and ease*

boost of dopamine. Grounding with the forest floor sends us a sense of warmth and connection as oxytocin elevates. Our pace slows down, breath softens, the body's tension eases and anxious thoughts grow quiet—cortisol and adrenaline drop while GABA and endorphins rise. These positive effects make forest bathing a powerful practice for supporting healthy neurotransmitter function and overall brain wellness.

a time to tune in to *kokoro*

My childhood was during a time of explosive economic growth in the city where I lived. I was surrounded by skyscrapers and neon lights, not forests and open skies. When the city was consumed by economic ambition, nature had no place in the equation, and I neither valued nor understood it. Back then, rural areas were viewed as the uncivilized fringe of a metropolis-chasing modernity. It wasn't until many years later, when I was burned out by the hectic urban lifestyle and the demands of my highly stressful banking job, that I began to appreciate nature.

I turned to nature for moments of solitude when I felt exhausted, breathless. I enjoyed going to the mountains near my home, wandering along the forest trails, touching trees, watching the dragonflies' agile wings flutter, and listening to the rivers' murmur. At my favorite sit spot, birds often appeared as if they came to keep me company, singing a new song to me every time. Being outdoors quieted the noise in my head, soothed my exhaustion, and gave me the space I didn't know I needed. Little by little, nature taught me how to breathe again. The forest reminded me that resilience isn't about pushing harder to meet the constant demands of work and life, that joy is not found in chasing achievements defined by society. It's about grounding myself, slowing down, taking breaks, and reconnecting with *kokoro*.

Shinrin-yoku is a sensory practice, but at its core it is a way of letting *kokoro* exhale. Among trees, we feel grounded, unhurried, and the heart-mind loosens. The forest reminds us of its slower heartbeat, and by stepping into it, you allow *kokoro* to realign its rhythm, letting life's energy sustain and thrive.

Forest bathing is a time to tune in to ourselves, to reconnect with our senses, and to communicate with nature. As a Certified Forest Bathing Guide, I guide each session through a series of "invitations" to participants (p. 61). The body is invited to slow down, and the parasympathetic nervous system kicks in, shifting the mind from "doing" into "being" mode. We listen to the wind swishing through the trees, feel the earth beneath our feet, touch

a tree, perhaps chat with a butterfly, and breathe in the forest air. We give ourselves permission to simply be present, to take pleasure in what nature offers to us.

There is no goal to achieve, no performance to measure, nothing to analyze. In this unhurried state, our senses awaken, we feel calmer and more grounded, and we come home to our body once again through a renewed connection with nature. Every session is unique: a different constellation of people, backgrounds, cultures, and genders coming together on that day at that time. Each session is shaped and guided by nature itself. It's not up to me to take control of the weather, or be fixated to a predetermined program, because Mother Nature will offer exactly the conditions needed for that session. I simply go with the flow, surrendering myself to be her instrument to carry messages she wants to share.

One of my most unforgettable encounters with nature happened in the *onsen* town of Kaga in Ishikawa Prefecture that nestles in the western coast of Honshu, the main island of Japan. It was a sunny afternoon in late November, the cold air still carried a taste of last night's heavy rain. After taking a soothing soak in a historical public bathhouse of the Yamashiro Onsen, I wandered through the quiet streets of this old town and soon found myself before Yakuoin Onsenji Temple, a sacred site built over 1,300 years ago to honor the guardian deities of the hot springs.

Climbing up the stone stairs, I entered a tranquil moss-covered garden with vibrant fall colors; I stood and observed ripples in the crystal-clear water of the pond, while the delicate Japanese maple leaves drifted onto a carpet of fiery red, gold, and copper fallen foliage. When I reached the top section of the temple, ancient trees stood tall and strong. One tree seemed to call to me. I approached, whispered a greeting, and asked permission to touch it. As my palms lightly pressed against the trunk, a current

of warm energy swirled around my icy fingers. Tears started running down my cheeks—what a delightful and peaceful surprise. In that moment, I felt an intimate connection with nature, an unspoken support offered to me, truly a gift that filled my heart with silent joy.

nature, humanity, and our future

Without even realizing it, many of us have drifted away from our ancestors' deep bond with the natural world. This separation is the root of the many challenges we face today: rising stress and loneliness, growing strain on our mental health, and the worsening damage to our ecosystems. The negative consequences ripple across humanity and the Earth. As rapid advances in technology and artificial intelligence (AI) continue to reshape our lives, the human–nature disconnection is likely to deepen further. The only hope for the future is to rekindle this lost bond.

The truth is, humans are part of the living world. We are intertwined with the forests, the waters, the soil, and the air.

When we forget this truth, we begin to behave as though we are above nature, or entitled to use it without respect. How can humanity be well when the planet is unwell? How can we thrive when water is polluted, crops are poisoned by chemicals, and livestock is raised in inhumane conditions?

To remain fully human, we must reawaken the senses to listen to birdsong, feel the wind, taste the soil, notice the changing colors, and dance with the seasons. Restoring this connection not only makes us feel good, but reminds us that this planet is our home, and together we must care for it and protect it.

Every person has played a part in the environmental harm we now witness, whether knowingly or not. Each of us holds a piece of the responsibility to repair what has been damaged. Restoration will take collective effort—individuals, communities, and nations, working side by side with humility, respect, and love for the more-than-human world.

As a fellow citizen of this beautiful Blue Planet, I feel a personal calling to be an ambassador for Mother Nature: to help people find their way back to her, to remember her beauty, her wisdom, and the remedies she offers. When we fall in love with her again, protection becomes instinctive. And through this shared love, we can begin to build a future where humanity and nature thrive together.

greening your home

Creating a forest-like sanctuary at home is one of the best ways to bond with nature. A few pots of indoor plants on the balcony or placed around a room will lighten up your home. Plants are a natural air purifier, disinfectant, and mood stabilizer. Spend time each day observing their life cycle, and converse with them too.

Fill your space with forest fragrance. I like diffusing *hinoki* or *hiba* (types of Japanese cypress) essential oils, as if I'm inside a Japanese forest. These oils contain a high content of phytoncides (p. 50) to benefit from inhaling the health-enhancing properties.

*"Here I sit
beneath a tree.
Heartbeat calm.
Soul hums free."*

Angie Weiland Crosby

nature as self-care

The forest is always waiting for you. You don't need to travel far or carve out much time to answer its call. You can enjoy this self-guided *shinrin-yoku* session alone or with a small group of friends, whether in a forest or a city park. Stay safe: be mindful of uneven ground, wildlife, and weather conditions, and choose places that feel familiar. To fully immerse yourself in nature, simply follow your intuition and devote the time to be present with yourself.

♦ Find a sit spot. Close your eyes and tune in to your body. Take a few moments to breathe and settle your mind.

♦ Spend 10–20 minutes to reflect upon each of the following invitations.

Invitation 1: Look for a nature object near you—a stone, a leaf, a branch. If there is anything preventing your presence here right now, leave it with this object.

Invitation 2: Connect with the environment. Look around, above, and below you, and begin to engage your senses. What do you hear, taste, see, and feel? Connect with the sky, the birds, the trees, the stones, and the soil.

Invitation 3: Wander around and find a nature object. Spend time observing it. What are its characteristics, pattern, texture, color, smell?

Invitation 4: If you feel comfortable walking barefoot, find somewhere suitable to do so. Feel the earth with every part of the soles of your feet. What do you notice?

Invitation 5: Spend time with a tree. Simply approach one that calls out to you. Greet the tree, it's your new friend. Hug it, touch it, have a conversation with it. Quiet your mind and listen to any messages it sends to you.

Invitation 6: Write a *haiku*—a short, simple Japanese poem, written in three lines of 5-7-5 syllables, though this pattern is not a strict rule. *Haikus* are often inspired by moments of observing nature. Writing a *haiku* is a wonderful way to express our sensory experiences during forest bathing. Below is a beautiful *haiku* that I love, written by a participant in one of my forest bathing sessions.

A stroll through the woods

Magical wands light up the path

My soul awakens

♦ Before leaving, give thanks to nature for the special moments you both shared together.

茶道

chadō (the way of tea)

For people in Japan, tea is an everyday companion. Green tea is often served upon sitting down at a restaurant. Bottles of tea fill vending machines, ready to be picked up at any time. At home, tea is prepared as the first warm drink in the morning, as a pause between tasks, or a quiet cup as the day settles. Tea is simply there at any moment of the day.

first bowl of tea in a humble teahouse

I vividly remember my first encounter with Japanese tea ceremony at Beniya Mukayu, a Zen-inspired contemporary *ryokan* in Yamashiro Onsen, Ishikawa Prefecture.

At the time, I didn't know that this moment would become the first of many encounters with tea, nor that it would never repeat itself in quite the same way again.

After check-in, my friend and I were invited to attend a traditional tea ceremony. We changed into *yukata*—the cotton robes worn at *onsen ryokan*—and were led through the Zen garden toward a small structure beneath old maple trees. It looked as though it belonged to the garden rather than asking to be noticed.

Inside, the space was unexpectedly spare. Plain, rustic, almost austere. The traditional tearoom was small—perhaps 4 ½ *tatami* mats—with very little light filtering through the *shoji* screens.

There were no ornaments, no decoration to catch the eye. Only the *tatami* floor, a sunken hearth, and the tea utensils laid out on the floor.

No one was there when we entered. The room was completely silent. We kneeled on the *tatami*, not knowing what would happen next, or when. Accustomed to being guided or instructed, we waited, unsure whether we were waiting correctly.

Several minutes later, a low sliding door on the side of the room opened. It was so small and close to the ground that we had not noticed it at all. A man entered by crouching through the opening, his movement deliberate and unhurried.

It was Mr. Nakamichi, the owner of Beniya Mukayu.

I didn't know then that he was a tea master. I felt instinctively the honor and the responsibility of being a guest, received with formality and humility.

He bowed. No words were spoken. In front of him were the tea utensils. He took a silk cloth from the belt of his *kimono* and began the ritual cleaning of the tea container and bamboo scoop. The bamboo whisk and tea bowl were warmed with water. Matcha powder was measured, hot water added, and the tea whisked into a soft green foam.

Each movement was gentle, precise, and unbroken by explanation—simply beautiful to watch.

Our legs began to tremble from kneeling, but we hesitated to move, unsure of what was permitted. Sensing this, Mr. Nakamichi gently invited us to sit more comfortably. His kind permission brought a wordless relief as we adjusted our posture with gratitude.

When the bowl of tea was offered, it was warm and fragrant. The matcha was creamy, slightly salty, bitter, and vivid in color. We drank quietly, holding the bowl with both hands, still unsure whether we were doing it correctly—and slowly realizing that correctness was not the point.

At the time, I knew none of the formal meanings embedded in the ceremony. I didn't know why utensils were cleaned in that precise way, or why the teahouse was so down-to-earth. Looking back, *chadō* began for me with not knowing. Only later did I begin to understand the depth, history, and grace of the Way of Tea.

Beniya Mukayu remains a place I return to, each stay recalling that first tea encounter, shared with Mr. Nakamichi and my friend. Years later, I learned that the old teahouse is no longer in use. The ceremony now takes place indoors. That gathering, in that small humble hut beneath the maple trees, exists only in memory.

Ichigo ichie.

One time, one meeting.

the roots of *chadō*, the way of tea

Because tea is everywhere, it is easy to forget that this ordinary drink carries centuries of practice.

Tea traveled to Japan from China with Buddhist monks in the eighth and ninth centuries, first used as a medicinal tonic and a ritual drink in temples and at court. In the late twelfth century, Zen priests introduced whisked powdered tea—what we now know as *matcha* (p. 70)—as a way to enable them to stay awake in their long hours of meditation.

In the late sixteenth century, Sen no Rikyū, the most influential Japanese tea master, transformed tea preparation into a profound art and way of living, defining *chadō*—the Way of Tea. He refined elaborate tea gatherings that had developed in earlier centuries into humbler practices aligned with Zen values. Seasonality, simplicity, and the ethic of treasuring each meeting were embodied in the restrained design of rustic teahouses. Through his influence, tea began to be practiced as a *dō*—a path or way—marking the emergence of its classic ceremonial expression. This "way" represents a lifelong discipline of self-cultivation where character is refined through practice.

Today, people often speak of *chadō*—the Way of Tea, while practitioners also use the older word *chanoyu*, often translated as the "tea ceremony," to refer to the act of preparing and sharing matcha. In *chanoyu*, the host and guest meet one another through something as modest as serving and receiving a bowl of matcha in a tearoom removed from ordinary busyness. Attention is directed away from performance and toward atmosphere, gesture, and relationship. Many gestures during *chanoyu* that now appear ritualized began as ordinary, practical tasks in Zen monasteries, refined into a form of care through time.

Tea masters expressed the heart of *chadō* through four guiding principles:

***Wa*, harmony:** Creating a gentle balance between people, space, and nature.

***Kei*, respect:** Meeting guests, objects, and the moment with sincere consideration.

***Sei*, purity:** Keeping body, utensils, and intention clean and uncluttered.

***Jaku*, tranquility:** The quiet, settled mind that emerges when the first three are lived fully.

These guide how tea is prepared, how guests are received, and how a single meeting is held as something that will never return in quite the same way.

ichigo ichie—one time, one meeting

How would you feel if this gathering, with this group of friends, this moment, never happens again?

In *chadō,* this feeling is expressed through the phrase *ichigo ichie*—"one time, one meeting." The tea ceremony becomes an aesthetic practice of meeting each unrepeatable moment with care. Even the simplest encounter is treated as once in a lifetime. To sit for tea with this awareness is to offer full attention to the present before it slips away.

This awareness guides the spirit of *omotenashi*—hospitality grounded in wholehearted care for the guest. Rather than a "service" the host provides, it is the thoughtful anticipation of what will make the encounter truly heartfelt. Long before guests arrive, the host prepares the gathering through the careful selection of tea, utensils, *kakemono* (hanging calligraphy scroll), and *wagashi* (seasonal sweets), each chosen to support the atmosphere of the moment. Guests arrive unaware of these preparations; they simply enter and allow the gathering to unfold. In a tearoom where words are few, tea becomes the language between host and guest, and the ceremony turns into a kind of meditation.

The teahouse itself supports *ichigo ichie*. Small and austere, it removes what is unnecessary so attention can rest fully in the present without distraction. Worn surfaces and uneven textures reflect a *wabi sabi* sensibility, where impermanence is not concealed and the passing nature of the moment remains visible.

Kisetsukan, a sense of the seasons, gives each "one time, one meeting" its particular flavor. It might appear in a seasonal flower arrangement, or in a *chawan* (tea bowl) that feels right for the weather. These details are subtle, gently reminding everyone that this meeting belongs to now, and only now. Seasonal awareness makes a tea gathering special, transforming a simple cup of tea into an immersive, aesthetic, and emotional celebration of the present moment.

Shizen, naturalness or non-forcing, keeps everything understated yet meaningful. Gestures are precise and smooth, refined by many years of practice, yet they do not look like a performance.

Together, these elements reinforce the spirit of *ichigo ichie*. Hospitality that does not show off, space that welcomes silence, attentiveness to the season, a natural manner, and a humble room, all

work in harmony to remind everyone present to cherish a moment that will not happen in quite the same way again.

With *ichigo ichie* in mind, how might you choose to meet the moments of everyday life that will not return?

the pratice of presence

Chadō is one of Japan's most refined arts to connect with *kokoro*. Every step is infused with attention and sincerity, drawing mind, body, and heart into what is happening now. The etiquette is a way to cultivate the inner state, letting outer order create inner order, and quiet gestures invite quietness within.

Japanese tea ceremony has become widely known outside Japan, often presented as an iconic cultural experience. For those experiencing *chadō* for the first time, once seated in the tearoom, they may feel puzzled as to how to respond. There is little verbal explanation, no narrative, only a series of deliberate actions to make a single bowl of tea.

Why devote so much time to something so quiet and restrained?

Why does a simple cup of tea require such ritualized procedure?

Used to efficiency, analysis, and stimulation, many approach tea with expectations that the practice does not seek to fulfill.

This challenge often stems from unfamiliarity with what it means to be fully present. Modern life rarely trains us to stay with one person, one action, one place. Attention is scattered. The mind is restless and unsettled, filled with mental chatter that shifts rapidly from thought to thought.

In this light, *chadō* can feel radical at first. Though it appears gentle and understated, it is a rigorous practice that requires discipline, restraint, and sustained attention. There is no shortcut, and very little variation. The movements are slow, the order fixed, the pauses intentional.

The practice of presence is most clearly embodied in *temae*—the ritualized way in which tea is prepared and served. *Temae* is not a performance, nor a technique aimed at efficiency. It is a form that holds attention, one gesture at a time. Folding the cloth, cleansing the scoop, warming the bowl, measuring the tea, lifting water with the ladle, whisking until the surface foams—each action is done at its own pace and weight. At first, these movements can feel like choreography to be memorized, but with repetition, they become a kind of moving meditation.

As guests, immersing our senses into every aspect of the tea ceremony is a practice of presence: watching the host's movements, noticing the warmth of the bowl, listening to the sound of whisking matcha, and bowing, turning the bowl, and tasting the tea with appreciation. These small rituals gently anchor the mind in the present.

kintsugi and *chadō*

I recognized a similar quality of attention during a *kintsugi* workshop. The repair of broken ceramics long predates *kintsugi*, or "golden joinery" (pp. 74–75), and can be traced to China, where restoration was mainly for durability rather than appearance. By the fifteenth century, however, visible repairs, often made with metal clamps, began to gain aesthetic value, symbolizing age and preciousness. These attitudes toward repair likely influenced Japanese aesthetic sensibilities in ceramic through extensive cultural exchange.

In Japan, restoration developed alongside the ethic of *mottainai*, the belief that objects should be well made, carefully maintained, and mended until they could no longer serve. *Shogun*, samurai, and tea masters often treated their favorite teabowls as irreplaceable companions—bowls were repaired rather than discarded when damaged.

Restoration techniques evolved from metal bracing and tar bonding toward methods using *urushi* lacquer, which had been used in Japan since ancient times as a strong adhesive. By the fifteenth century, lacquer repair had become refined in the cultural context of tea.

The development of *kintsugi* as an art form is closely tied to *chadō*. As tea culture shifted toward rustic and modest vessels, signs of wear and repair were embraced rather than concealed. *Kintsugi*, using *urushi* lacquer finished with powdered gold or other metals, allowed tea utensils to remain in use while openly displaying their history. Within *chadō*, repaired ceramics came to embody continuity, care, and the passage of time—qualities central to tea practice.

lessons from practicing *kintsugi*

Although I had heard about *kintsugi* for years and admired repaired bowls in small ceramic shops around Japan, it was not until a visit to Fukuoka that I had the opportunity to feel the process with my own hands. I enrolled in a private workshop with Mikki Tam, a Japan-based designer and social entrepreneur who dedicates her work to sustaining Japan's disappearing rural craft traditions.

Before the repair work began, Mikki shared the historical background of *kintsugi*, clarifying misconceptions that have become common today. Because traditional repairs take weeks or months to complete, she had prepared pieces at different stages so I could experience the full sequence within a single workshop. The process was fascinating. Rejoining fragments demanded precision and calm. With one bowl, we cleaned and adhered the fragments using *urushi* lacquer mixed with wheat flour and wood powder. With another, we filled gaps and rebuilt a missing section, reinforcing with hemp fiber. Only at the very end did I touch the part most people associate with *kintsugi*: dusting the surface with fine metal powder, and gently polishing the soft golden line.

What struck me most was the meticulous, almost meditative nature of the work. While the golden seams often receive the most attention, I found the less visible earlier stages far more intriguing. The restoration depends not only on the skills of the craftsmen, but also on a network of artisans whose work remains largely unseen: *urushi* tree farmers, brush makers, paper makers, clay manufacturers, goldsmiths. Without their behind-the-scenes contributions, the repair could not exist.

Of all the steps, filling the gaps was the most challenging, particularly when layering hemp fiber to support bigger missing parts. The process cannot be rushed. Each layer must dry fully before the next can be applied. My hands felt clumsy, but I realized that precision was less important than attention. It was my first experience and simply staying present with the work was enough.

This resonated deeply with *chadō*, where what matters most is sincere presence with what is in front of you. The much-lauded gold is only a thin line on top of years of skill, many layers of lacquer, and the hands of makers whose names are rarely spoken. Like the preparations before a tea gathering, their work remains intentionally out of view. Both *kintsugi* and *chadō* remind us that what appears effortless is sustained by devoted, invisible effort, and that true beauty arises from meeting each moment, each break, each repair, and each bowl of tea as a once-in-a-lifetime encounter.

invitation to tea rituals at home

Chadō is a lifelong practice shaped through years of study. What follows is not a tea ceremony, but a simple way of inviting the spirit of tea into everyday life.

When you participate in tea, *kokoro* is invited into a space of harmony (*wa*), respect (*kei*), purity (*sei*), and tranquility (*jaku*). As the body learns these qualities, they begin to weave into how you move, not just in the tearoom but beyond it.

PREPARING A BOWL OF MATCHA (*USUCHA*)

This simple preparation follows the traditional method for usucha*, or thin matcha. It can be practiced as a quiet daily ritual, offering a moment to slow down and attend to what is present. You'll need:*

2 g matcha powder (about 1½ heaped bamboo scoops or 1 level teaspoon)

¼ cup (60 ml) of hot water (about 176°F/80°C—not boiling)

a tea bowl* (chawan*)

a bamboo whisk* (chasen*)

a fine sieve (optional, but recommended)

Sift the matcha Place the matcha into the *chawan* through a fine sieve to remove any clumps. This helps the tea whisk smoothly and evenly.

Add hot water Pour ¼ cup (60 ml) of hot water at approximately 175°F (80°C) into the *chawan*. If the water has just boiled, allow it to cool briefly before using.

Whisk the tea Use the *chasen* to whisk briskly for about 15 seconds. Move the whisk back and forth in a gentle "M" or "W" motion until the surface becomes lightly frothy.

Pause and drink When the foam settles evenly across the surface, the tea is ready. Lift the bowl, take a moment to notice its warmth and color, and drink the tea while it is fresh.

A SIMPLE TEA RITUAL (WITHOUT MATCHA)

This ritual captures some of the spirit of chadō using what you already have. A single cup, prepared with care, is enough. You'll need:

loose-leaf tea or a tea bag, choose a tea you enjoy, green, black, herbal—there is no wrong choice here

hot water

a mug or cup

a kettle

Prepare the space Before you begin, take a moment to clear the surface where you will make your tea. Place your cup there deliberately. This small act marks the beginning of the ritual.

Heat the water Bring fresh water to a boil, then let it rest briefly if you are making green or delicate tea. The water should be hot, but not harsh. This pause matters.

Add the tea Place the loose leaves or tea bag into your cup. Notice the texture, the scent, the weight of it in your hand.

Pour and wait Pour the hot water over the tea. As it steeps, do not rush to fill the time. Let the leaves open, the water change color, the warmth rise from the cup.

Steep for a few minutes, depending on the tea, then remove the leaves or tea bag when the time feels right.

Sit with the tea Before drinking, pause. Hold the cup with both hands if you like. Feel its warmth. Take a breath. Then drink slowly, without distraction.

These simple tea practices allow you to meet this moment fully. The care you bring to making an ordinary cup becomes the care you offer yourself.

Tea is one way of practicing presence, but not the only one. Wherever attention is given with care, even an everyday activity can return to presence.

座禅

zazen (zen meditation)

Zazen is commonly translated into English as Zen meditation. Yet, in many other forms of meditation, the mind is actively engaged with a specific aim: focusing on the breath, setting an intention, observing thoughts, chanting a mantra, or visualizing a scene. *Zazen* offers a different orientation.

what is *zazen*?

Zazen is not easily grasped through explanation. For many, the word feels vague or even incomprehensible at first. Is it a meditation technique? A religious ritual? A way to calm the mind? Like many aspects of Zen, *zazen* is best approached not as a concept to understand, but as a practice to be met directly.

Zazen has been the core practice of Zen Buddhism for centuries. The word *za* means sitting, so *zazen* literally means "seated Zen". It emerged from the broader Buddhist meditation traditions that traveled from India to China, where seated practice was seen as a central part of the path toward enlightenment. In the thirteenth century, the Japanese Zen master Dōgen Zenji traveled to China to study Buddhism. Upon returning to Japan, he profoundly reshaped how *zazen* is understood and practiced.

Rather than treating *zazen* as a preparation for enlightenment, Dōgen viewed it as the direct embodiment of awakening itself—the unity of practice and realization. Awakening is not something that comes later as a result of effort, it is expressed simply by

"Zazen practice is the direct expression of our true nature."

Shunryū Suzuki

sitting wholeheartedly in this very posture and breath, as the original wholeness of one's own mind.

In Zen, *zazen* is not practiced as a meditation technique or mental exercise for shaping the mind, nor as a way to achieve a particular experience. It is practiced as *shikantaza*, or "just sitting", without a goal, without an object of attention, and without striving for attainment. One simply sits with an upright posture, breathes naturally, and allows thoughts, sensations, and feelings to arise and pass away without control or judgment. Experience is allowed to unfold exactly as it is.

Zen teachers have treated this plain act of sitting as the very heart of their path, the place where everything else begins and returns. To be alive here and now is the fundamental truth of our life. Zen refers to this as the original self, and *zazen* is the practice of sitting as this truth.

This understanding sets Zen apart from ways of practice that treat meditation as a tool for self-improvement or spiritual progress. *Zazen* makes no promise of calm or certainty and does not seek specific outcomes. It is less something we do and more a way of being. By releasing goals and expectations, the practice becomes an invitation to sit in pure stillness and encounter life exactly as it is.

body and mind as one

In much of Western culture, body and mind are treated as separate entities. The mind is often seen as the center of thought and identity, while the body is viewed as a mechanical structure. By contrast, in many Eastern traditions, including Zen, body and mind are regarded as a single, integrated whole, inseparable in lived experience.

Zazen is grounded in this understanding of unity. It is not a mental discipline layered on top of physical stillness, but an embodied practice in which body and mind settle together into a unified way of being.

shoshin—the beginner's mind

Much of our way of living is conditioned by instructions, and the desire to achieve the best possible results. We are taught that the more we know, the better we perform; the more information we gather, the more confident and successful we become. From this mindset, it is natural to want clear answers: What steps should I take to become good at *zazen*? What more do I need to know? How long will it take to reach the next level?

Perhaps we may read more books or ask more questions, hoping to gain enough information to feel prepared. But in *zazen*, instructions are minimal and simple. The practice asks for a very

different quality of mind—one that is open, receptive, and unburdened by accumulated ideas, beliefs, and expectations. This attitude of meeting each moment freshly and without bias is called *shoshin*, or "beginner's mind."

"If you start to practice zazen, *you will begin to appreciate your beginner's mind. It is the secret of Zen practice."*

Shunryū Suzuki

Zazen is a continuous process of direct and honest experience approached each time with beginner's mind. It is not attached to goals, expectations, fixed ideas, or judgments of right and wrong. In Zen teachings, the original mind is boundless and already sufficient; beginner's mind is how this original mind reveals itself in practice—open, curious, and free of fixed ideas. When we bring expectations or rigid ideas to *zazen*, we narrow this openness and limit possibilities in life.

Posture forms the foundation of this practice. When the body is settled in a stable, upright, and relaxed way, the mind naturally reflects the same balance. Sitting on a chair or cushion with the pelvis grounded, spine lengthened, shoulders relaxed, chin gently tucked, and hands resting in a *mudra* (a hand gesture commonly used in meditation) creates a posture that supports a clear state of mind. If we slump, the mind tends toward dullness; if we strain, the mind becomes tense and effortful. The "right" posture is not rigid or perfect, but one in which body and mind feel supported and breathing flows at ease.

mushin—no mind

When we repeatedly return to beginner's mind and let thoughts and feelings pass without engaging them, this is called *mushin*, or no mind—a mind not owned or dominated by thoughts. Body sensations, emotions, and ideas arise and dissolve on their own. In the absence of attachment, reactivity, and excessive conceptual thinking, the mind becomes transparent and fluid, capable of responding naturally to circumstances because body and mind are no longer divided.

This unity may resemble what is often called a *flow state*—a condition in which the mind is fully present and the body responds with natural precision and ease. In Zen, however, this is not a state to pursue. It is a natural expression of ourselves when distractions fall away.

"You might drop into a flow state while sitting, and gradually, that same clarity starts to appear in ordinary moments. You come home, start cooking or cleaning, and think... this feels like I was sitting zazen. *That sense of stillness stays with you."*

Daichi Isokawa

With time, we begin to embody the practice of *zazen* in daily life. We may listen more fully, act with less hesitation, and feel less divided between what we think and what we do. As body and mind integrate in the stillness of sitting, we return to *kokoro*—the living heart-mind where thought, feeling, intuition, and sensitivity meet. From here, we can be true to what we feel and respond to life with greater warmth and clarity.

just being yourself, sitting in stillness

Modern life trains us to move with purpose. We are taught that value comes from planning and doing—analyzing, setting goals, and steering our lives toward measurable outcomes. The mind is rarely allowed to rest. Time becomes precious, not a moment can be spared for doing nothing. For some people, silence and stillness can even feel uncomfortable or lonely.

From this mindset, *zazen*'s invitation to "just sit, be yourself, and let things be as they are" can sound like the opposite of common sense. It is natural to meet the practice with questions about purpose and results: Why do nothing if nothing is being achieved? What does this practice actually do? How can sitting quietly on a cushion help us?

- Zen is the practice of accepting things as they are.
- No need to empty the mind to practice *zazen*.
- No need to be calm or spiritual.
- Just be yourself, sitting in stillness.
- Thoughts will rise and settle in their own time.

Zazen offers a deliberate pause. Rather than promising transformation through effort, it takes us back to what is already present. It invites us to step beyond goals and outcomes, to encounter a different way of being. This presence is cultivated through three fundamental relationships:

Posture: Harmonizing the relationship with the ground.

Breathing: Harmonizing the relationship with the air.

Mental state: Harmonizing the relationship with sensory experience.

By sitting still, upright, and present without a goal, we directly experience breathing, sensing, and being aware—right here, right now. This is an act of returning to our true nature, or true self. As we meet experience honestly and without judgment, the capacity of *kokoro* opens. The mind loosens its grip on control and stops organizing life around success or failure. From this openness, compassion naturally arises as the heart's response, guiding how we meet whatever appears—fear, sadness, happiness, desire. Our sense of self becomes broader and more fluid, less confined to who we think we should be, and more able to meet life's circumstances with a connected, spacious presence.

Zen does not deny the usefulness of planning or effort. These abilities are essential in daily life. But when every moment is treated as a problem to solve or a target to reach, experience narrows. *Zazen* is not an escape from modern life, rather, it teaches us how to meet life without being consumed by it. As we learn to trust reality as it unfolds, effort becomes responsive rather than forced, and clarity and compassion begin to guide our actions.

the practice

"The purpose of our practice is to open up our mind." **Shunryū Suzuki**

In the context of self-care, *zazen* offers a way of re-entering life more fully. As we practice sitting in stillness, we begin to notice signs of exhaustion or misalignment with our deeper needs. Gradually, we learn to inhabit our lives from inside out, rather than constantly pushing forward from the surface.

Zazen begins with the simplest elements: how we sit, how we breathe, and how we receive the world through our senses. As Zen priest Isshō Fujita explains, sitting with good posture means aligning ourselves with gravity rather than struggling against it. The lower body settles fully into the support of the floor while the upper body remains open, relaxed, and aware, as if gently suspended from above.

Breathing is natural and unforced. With our senses—eyes, ears, nose, tongue, body, and mind—softened and at ease, we simply receive each moment of experience, letting practice become a wordless dialogue between body, breath, and mind.

prepare the space and body

Choose a quiet, clean corner where you will not be disturbed.

Wear loose, comfortable clothing. Silence your phone, avoid sitting right after heavy meals or drinking alcohol.

Choose your seat

On a cushion:

- Use a firm cushion, sit on the front half, hips slightly higher than knees.
- Let both knees touch the floor or a mat for stability.
- If comfortable, sit in lotus position: place the right foot onto your left thigh and left foot onto your right thigh.

On a chair:

- Sit toward the front edge with both feet flat on the floor, knees about hip-width apart.
- Avoid leaning back, if possible let your spine support itself.

Find your posture

- Sit upright but not stiff, as if the crown of your head is gently lifting toward the ceiling.
- Let the lower back maintain its natural curve, the chest soft and shoulders relaxed.
- Tuck your chin slightly so the neck lengthens.
- Gently sway side to side and front to back until you find a sense of balance.

Hands, eyes, mouth

- Hands: rest them in your lap, right hand palm up, left hand on top, thumbs lightly touching to form a soft oval.
- Mouth: close your mouth, tongue resting lightly against the roof just behind the teeth.
- Eyes: keep them half-open, gaze lowered to the floor without focusing on anything.

Breathe naturally

- Take one or two slightly deeper breaths to settle.
- Then let the breath return to its natural rhythm, in and out through the nose.
- Feel the breath in the lower belly.

Relating to thoughts and feelings

- There is no need to stop thoughts. Simply notice when attention wanders.
- Each time you realize you are thinking, gently return to posture and breath.
- Allow thoughts, emotions, and sensations to pass through like weather, without chasing or resisting them.

Ending the sit

- When your sitting time is up, remain aware of the body and avoid standing abruptly.
- Bring your hands together briefly, then rest them on your thighs.
- Gently sway side to side, then slowly uncross your legs or move your feet.
- Stand up carefully, take a few slow, mindful steps before returning to your day.

remembering *noto* through *zazen*

I visited the Noto Peninsula in Ishikawa Prefecture (above left) in late fall of 2022. Sitting *zazen* at Meikizan Taiseiin temple was part of a homestay program run by elderly locals who open their homes now that their children have grown up and moved to the cities. During my stay, I understood barely half of the conversations with my host parents in Japanese. We relied on smiles, nods, small gestures, and the help of translation tools. Even so, I clearly felt how deeply the community was rooted in Noto—in the land, the sea, the temple, and one another.

My host family drove us along quiet rural roads, passing rice fields and low wooded hills. Near the entrance stood a tall, narrow wooden pillar inscribed with vertical brushed Chinese characters. Inside, my two friends and I were greeted by the Zen priest who would guide the *zazen* session. He led us into the temple hall, where three cushions had been arranged on the floor. I briefly wondered, almost amused, whether he might carry a long stick sometimes used in temples to correct posture, but he didn't. He gave simple instructions in Japanese, which I was able to follow, explaining how to sit upright and how to arrange our legs in the lotus position, which felt natural to me.

We sat for about thirty minutes—just sitting, breathing naturally. During the practice, he quietly observed us and gently corrected our posture when we began to slump. Thoughts arose from time to time, but I noticed them and let them pass. When the session ended, my body and senses felt calm and settled, and we shared tea and sweets outside the hall. This was the kind of temple no tourist would stumble upon without being brought there by the people of Noto, which made the experience feel much more intimate and grounded.

After the devastating Noto earthquake on New Year's Day in 2024, I often found myself thinking of the Noto community and the temple. I wondered whether the home I stayed in was still standing, whether my host parents were safe, whether people could still gather at the temple. *Zazen* continues beyond the moment of sitting. The stillness experienced on the cushion remains, reminding me that our shared humanity and connection live in *kokoro*, even across distance.

if you're wondering about *zazen*...

♦ Do I need to stop my thoughts to practice *zazen*?
No. zazen *does not ask you to stop thinking.*

Thoughts will arise. In zazen, *this is not a problem or a sign that you are doing it wrong. Thoughts are treated as part of what is happening, not as something to control or eliminate. When you notice you have been carried away by thinking, simply return to sitting. Not to fix anything, but to resume being here.*

♦ If I'm not focusing on anything, what am I supposed to do?
You are not asked to do anything in the usual sense.

Zazen *is not about directing attention toward an object, such as the breath, a word, or a visualization. The posture itself becomes the practice. Sitting upright, breathing naturally, and staying present are enough.*

When you notice you've wandered, you return not to a task, but to sitting.

♦ Is *zazen* the same as mindfulness meditation?
They are related, but not the same.

Many mindfulness practices involve actively observing thoughts, sensations, or emotions. Zazen *does not require observation as a task. There is no instruction to watch the mind or label experience. In* zazen, *awareness is allowed to function without being directed.*

♦ What if I feel restless, bored, or uncomfortable?
That is part of zazen.

Zazen *includes the experience of restlessness, boredom, discomfort, calm, ease, and everything in between. It does not aim to replace one experience with another. Rather than trying to escape discomfort or wait for something better to happen,* zazen *invites you to stay with kindness and steadiness. If pain or discomfort becomes overwhelming, you are encouraged to adjust your posture or stop.* Zazen *is not about endurance or forcing yourself.*

♦ How long should I sit?
Short and consistent is better than long and occasional.

It is recommended to practice sitting zazen *for 20 minutes or longer. The quality of sitting matters more than duration.* Zazen *is not measured by time, depth, or intensity. After practicing for a while, the duration will gradually increase without realizing it.*

♦ Is it okay to practice *zazen* in a chair?
Yes.

Zazen *is about upright, balanced sitting—not about achieving a specific pose. A chair can support a stable and attentive posture just as well as a cushion on the floor.*

Comfort and steadiness matter more than form.

◆ What if I don't feel calm or peaceful afterward?
Zazen *does not promise calm.*

Sometimes sitting feels grounding or quiet. Sometimes it feels busy or unsettled. Zazen *does not judge either experience as better or worse. With time, many people notice a greater capacity to stay present with whatever arises—but this is not something to expect or demand.*

◆ Is *zazen* a form of relaxation?
Zazen *may feel relaxing at times, but relaxation is not its goal, and there is no goal in the practice.* Zazen *is a way of meeting experience honestly, not a method for producing a particular state. If relaxation comes, it comes. If it does not, the practice continues.*

◆ What if I'm doing it wrong?
If you are sitting and returning, you are practicing zazen.

There is no perfect posture, no ideal mental state, and no correct experience to achieve. Zazen *is not about getting it right, it is about staying.*

◆ Do I need to believe in Buddhism to practice *zazen*?
No.

Zazen *does not require belief. It is a practice of sitting and presence that can be entered directly, without adopting a philosophy or worldview. You are invited to try it and see what unfolds.*

chapter 3

for the soul

CARE FOR THE BODY GROUNDS US and connection with the mind centers us. As we travel inward and reach the deeper layer of our being, nurturing the soul is what makes us whole. In Japanese culture, the soul, also *kokoro*, often reveals itself in the small, sincere moments that remind us of who we are.

Well-being of the soul is not about purity, perfection, or spiritual achievement. Caring for the soul is found in the ordinary grace of decluttering, honoring imperfections, and finding purpose in the everyday.

This final chapter invites you to nurture *kokoro*, to look inward with honesty and without judgment, healing the quietest part of yourself so you can return to the self your *kokoro* recognizes as home.

放下著

hogejaku **(letting go)**

To live in the spirit of *hogejaku*, a Zen expression that literally means "to let go" or "to throw away," we must look at simplifying the material world, making peace with change, and releasing emotions that hinder our growth or harm our health. The Zen ideas of non-attachment, impermanence, simplicity, and spaciousness will help you release what you no longer need to carry.

the zen way of letting go

"Let things go and your life will improve," says Shunmyo Masuno, the head priest of a 450-year-old Zen Buddhist temple in Japan. In daily life, we accumulate objects, thoughts, and emotional residue without noticing. Liberation comes with the willingness to put something down, which often begins in ordinary moments. Perhaps it's an old object you haven't touched in years, one that sends shivers down your spine. As it leaves your grip, the chest loosens, like an old knot beginning to untie. In this stillness, it is a gentle, fearless letting go of what has already finished in your life. Not erasing the past, but opening a space in your *kokoro* when you stop holding what no longer serves. This is the essence of *hogejaku*.

When we refer to letting go in everyday life, it is about changing our relationship with people, things, experiences, or thoughts. In Zen, *mushūchaku*, meaning "non-attachment," teaches us that to release is to let the experience arise and pass freely. We are free to be joyful and free to be sad, yet we do not cling to these feelings in ways that prevent us from moving on.

It is the practice of meeting each moment with openness and acknowledging that things and people change over time. When we give ourselves permission to release, we discover that we are not losing anything essential, but rather letting light into *kokoro* to guide us toward a more fruitful future.

why we hold on

In my coaching practice, I often meet people who hold on to objects, habits, roles, or relationships because they feel comfortably familiar. A bad habit can offer comfort, a mundane job can feel reassuringly stable, possessions can signal success, or expectations can make the world more predictable. Letting go often feels insecure because we are stepping outside of our comfort zone—even when something no longer fits who we are, parting with it can feel like closing a chapter we're not quite ready to finish. And sometimes, holding on is simply easier than making a decision, so we bargain with ourselves: "maybe I'll need this one day," "maybe I'll regret it if I quit," or "I'll deal with it later." The practice of *hogejaku* begins with noticing these attachments, acknowledging that they no longer define us, having the courage to detach and change, and eventually choosing what truly supports the life you want to live.

Attachment to small things. There is always something small to shed each day. *Hogejaku* applies just as much to the lighter clutter of daily life as to the heaviest chapters of our story. By regularly removing what is no longer needed, we prevent it from piling up in *kokoro* and avoid those overwhelming, once-in-a-long-time "clearouts" that make parting with things feel more difficult. When we reconcile with ourselves in this ongoing manner, lightness in *kokoro* becomes a daily experience rather than an occasional reset.

Attachment to emotions. Everyday feelings naturally rise and fall. But when we cling to irritation, replay small frustrations, or carry the weight of a single comment for days, we turn short-lived emotions into long-term burdens. In Zen, to "be of one essence" teaches us that the body, mind, and heart move together instead of in different directions. We let emotions move through life as one flowing experience rather than build homes inside us—to acknowledge them, allow them, and let them pass.

Attachment to opinions. Sometimes, we adhere firmly to our views and opinions and refuse to stay open-minded on dissimilarities. When a belief becomes rigid, the mind closes; when the mind closes, life narrows. Worse still, rigidity in our own beliefs can lead us to judge others unfairly. Our perspectives are shaped by our experiences, and experiences evolve. What we believed at 20 may not serve us at 40. *Mushūchaku* allows us to update who we are without shame.

Differences in background and viewpoint naturally create friction. Holding on to disagreement, rejection, or resentment tightens the *kokoro* and drains our energy. *Yurusu*, or forgiveness, opens the mind to become generous enough to let things be, even though we may not understand or agree with others.

Attachment to identities and relationships. Perhaps the most delicate form of attachment is clinging to identities and relationships. We hold on to who we once were because it feels safer than stepping into who we are becoming. We dwell in past glories or weaknesses, but forget it's possible to shape ourselves with equal beauty and grace as life moves on. We hold on to people because their presence once stabilized us, but forget that they, too, change.

Zen teaches us *mujo*, meaning "impermanence"—the recognition that everything is in motion and clinging to things leads to dissatisfaction or suffering. When we accept this natural flow of change, inner hardness softens,

and *kokoro* can guide us back to peace with our evolving identities and relationships.

zen minimalism—simplicity is freedom from excess

Simplicity sounds effortless, yet in the age of constant innovation, it is not that simple. Technology claims to ease our lives, but in reality it often adds new layers of complication: endless updates, constant notifications, more noise. Living simply now requires a conscious practice to turn away from excess.

This does not mean we need to abandon technology or resist efficiency, or try to go back in time and replicate ancient lifestyles. The real problem is that modern life dazzles us with too many choices, distracting us from what we truly need. The continuous feed of commercials, algorithmic advertisements, and social media featuring the latest models of things confuses us into thinking that these are necessities, giving us more reasons to buy. Gradually, the insatiable greed and boundless desire take over our minds.

Yet the paradox remains: the more things we own, the more those things begin to own our time, our attention, and our sense of self. Underneath the desire for more often lies something deeper: insecurity, loneliness, or a longing for refuge. But objects can only offer superficial-level comfort for a brief moment; they cannot fill the spaces inside us that require presence rather than possession.

We can turn to a Zen minimalism way of living to seek both inner and outer freedom. Beyond being merely a contemporary design trend, this simplicity has been cultivated in Zen monasteries for centuries to support spiritual focus. Monks strip their surroundings down to the bare minimum in order not to be distracted. Over time, this discipline evolved into a classical aesthetic principle of *kanso*, or "simplicity," often exhibited as clean, subtle design in architecture, tea rooms, and gardens. In *kanso*, the essential becomes the focal point of a Zen space, undisturbed by the visual noise of the excess: a living expression of "less is more."

"Those who know sufficiency are rich in spirit, even if they own little."

Dōgen Zenji

How can we put simplicity into our daily living? One approach is the Japanese concept of *danshari*, the lifestyle practice of refusing the unnecessary, discarding the excess, and separating from the emotional attachment to possessions. Practicing simplicity has become a modern skill to let us distinguish the essential from the nice-to-have. It is also a powerful way to support environmental sustainability by reducing waste and overconsumption.

Minimalism helps us become more aware of how much we allow possessions and innovations to shape us, or even control us. It reminds us to return to the basics that reflect ancient wisdom and values, human rhythm, and genuine sufficiency. The simplest essentials are more than enough to nourish us and anchor us in a life of meaning, within a world of abundance. After all, we really don't need much to live well. A *kokoro* filled with simplicity desires nothing more.

the body remembers—releasing trapped emotions

There is a quiet intelligence in the body. Even when the mind has moved on, the body keeps a record. It remembers the clenching of the jaw when a situation felt uncertain, the heaviness in the heart during grief. These patterns often hide away the unexpressed feelings and burdens, silently shaping the way we think and behave. They settle into the *kokoro* like stones, holding us down, making it harder to breathe, move, and carry on our lives.

Modern somatic understanding suggests that stress, unspoken emotions, and even long-ago hurts often manifest as body pain, shallow breathing rhythms, and poor posture. In my work as a Gyrotonic Trainer guiding clients' movement, I've learned that the body is an extraordinary system always doing its best to keep us safe at all times, but it can also become overwhelmed. The body never lies; it speaks to us in its

own language. Posture and movement reveal stories and truths that words often hide: a lifted shoulder or a hunched back reveal the tension someone carries from ongoing work stress; a person recovering from a hyperventilation incident may feel blockage in the chest that makes each inhale shallow; and sometimes a simple stretch can bring tears when emotions have been waiting for permission to be released.

In my own healing journey, I was deeply moved by the work of Mariko Hiyama, a Japanese face reflexologist who specializes in Facial Reflex Therapy for holistic healing. I realized how eloquently the face can reveal a landscape of reflex zones that mirror the organs, nervous system, and meridian pathways. The method stimulates the nervous system and supports balance in the body and mind. Each reflex point serves as a doorway to release long-forgotten feelings and memories. Mariko calls her approach "*te a te*" in Japanese, meaning "healing through touch." It is a beautiful integration of face reflexology, aromatherapy, and Japanese *kampo* (traditional Japanese herbal medicine).

During the session, her hands moved softly across my face, pausing at pressure points that felt strangely tender. Very quickly, I was immersed in a state of deep relaxation, like being half asleep. When the gentle sound of chimes woke me after the session was finished, an hour had passed and I felt a sense of relief and calmness. There was clarity in my head and lightness in my heart. Trapped emotions that had been held in the tissues were finally let go. What looks like a simple facial treatment turned out to be a deeply therapeutic emotional release.

Mariko Hiyama was born and raised in Fukuoka of Kyushu Island. Her work takes root in the memory of her grandmother's warm hands easing her aches in childhood, a touch that carried invisible healing. Although she once pursued business studies in Luxembourg with the intention of becoming an entrepreneur, Mariko witnessed the reality behind corporate success. She saw business leaders living with unhealthy lifestyles, chronic stress, exhaustion, and emotional disconnection. This realization led her to become a therapist instead, dedicating her hands to healing people. She has brought this amazing therapy to wellness resorts around the world, supporting people in letting go of their heaviness in *kokoro*—this is *hogejaku* in service of holistic well-being.

releasing with *hogejaku*—a self-care practice

decluttering your home

Practice *danshari*—refuse, dispose, separate—with this Zen-inspired decluttering exercise.

- **Set an intention before you start.**
- **Choose one small zone of your home (e.g. a desk or a cabinet).**
- **As you look through the items, consider the following:**

Do similar items keep appearing?
If yes, discard it.

Does this item still serve me well?
Will I miss anything if I eliminate it?
If no, discard it.

Review items eliminated from above, and set a goal to separate yourself from these items to avoid accumulation in the future.

- **Sort the discarded items into three bags: donation, recycling, and trashing.**
- **Try practicing *kanso* to keep the area as simple and clean as possible from now on.**

releasing your negative emotions

Negative emotions such as shame, guilt, apathy, grief, fear, and anger can impair our well-being. Practices such as deep breathing, meditation, sound therapy, and movement can help clear negative emotions from the body. Renewing your mind regularly is the best way to avoid their accumulating, so make it a daily habit to dedicate time to shedding them.

- **Practice deep breathing:**

At the end of each day, practice deep breathing. Set an intention first, then start with five minutes, and slowly increase the duration. Focus on inhaling the positive thoughts or happy moments, and exhaling all worries and negative energy of the day. Doing this before going to bed will prepare your body and mind for a deeper, better quality of sleep.

- **Practice meditation and sound healing:**

Refer to the *zazen* self-care ritual for seated meditation practice (pp. 86–87).

Or, try a meditation app. Nowadays, there are many that are freely available. Most of them have great choices of guided meditation and sound baths. Choose one that suits your need of the day.

Sound is a great way to unwind the mind and shift the brain's frequency into a more relaxed state. You can listen to soothing music anytime and anywhere, or join a sound-healing session like singing bowls, gongs, or chimes offered at wellness studios.

◆ Practice moving the body:
Movement helps the body release trapped emotions. Besides, exercise promotes the release of dopamine and strengthens the mind-body connection.

Unlike high-intensity exercises that may increase the release of stress hormones, movement disciplines such as Yoga, Pilates, and Gyrotonic foster somatic awareness and mindfulness. They are more body-mind-centered with mindful breathing techniques that support the body in letting go of tension and trapped emotions stored in muscles and fascia.

It is not ideal to do an intense evening workout as the body needs to begin winding down. Exercise is beneficial, but doing so after sunset keeps the body in a heightened state that disrupts sleep. Respect your body clock; choose a form of movement that follows the rhythms of the day in support of your well-being.

reviewing your relationships

By observing our connections with honesty and kindness, we release assumptions and old perceptions and open space for deeper self-respect and healthier relationships. This self-reflection practice helps to realign and guide us back to relationships that feel more grounded and true.

◆ Review relationship with self:
What judgments about myself have I been repeating for years, and are they still true in this season of my life?

In what ways have I already changed, and how can I honor this change instead of clinging to an old version of myself?

When discomfort arises in me: do I immediately label it as "bad," or can I stay curious about what it is trying to show me?

Which assumptions about my limits might actually be old protective stories, no longer needed now?

◆ Review relationship with others:
What fixed stories do I carry about others, and how might they be limiting my ability to see who they are now?

What assumptions and judgments about others have I made that can be let go? Am I willing to listen with fresh ears and an open heart?

How have others changed over time, and am I allowing space for that change, or relating to an older version of them?

Have I held grudges against anyone? Can I open my heart to forgive them?

Can I accept differences with others—in values, choices, or paths—without immediately trying to fix, correct, or convince?

If I viewed this relationship as a mirror, which of my rigid beliefs is it inviting me to soften or release?

侘寂

wabi sabi **(perfectly imperfect)**

Wabi sabi did not begin as a celebration of imperfection. In fact, the two words were originally not understood as a pair, and both carried rather negative meanings. "The idea of *wabi* means insufficiency—physically lacking something; mentally, it refers to a dire situation, the worst possible condition," said Dairik Amae, a tea practitioner and teacher based in Kyoto. *Sabi*, on the other hand, originally described the way things deteriorate with time, evoking desolation and decay.

the gift of being perfectly imperfect

Most of us own something that is not quite perfect.

A soft toy with faded colors and broken stitches.

An out-of-fashion handbag gifted by your father when you were a child.

A chipped mug you've kept since your college days.

They carry meaning for us, they remind us of moments we have lived through, they give us comfort. In their imperfections, they feel more real than anything new and polished. As they age, they are even more cherished. In Japanese, this instinct to love the unpolished, the uneven, and the aged is the concept of *wabi sabi.*

Through lived experience and the influence of Zen Buddhism, the meaning of *wabi* gradually evolved from suffering

"Wabi sabi is an intuitive response to beauty that reflects the true nature of life."

Beth Kempton

caused by lack to an acceptance of simplicity, and *sabi* shifted to express beauty revealed through aging and the passage of time. Eventually, the two words came together as *wabi sabi,* reflecting a time-honored appreciation for things that are modest, weathered, and unfinished.

It is an underlying sensibility presented through art, space, and perception—often appearing as an unpolished and austere design style that is not meant to impress, but to honestly express reality. These elements naturally enhance the object's own character, treating it as a companion in daily life rather than a piece that demands attention.

In the same way, appreciating *wabi sabi* reminds us that life is never meant to be perfect. It inspires us to value the ordinary rhythm of life, and to reframe our perception so we can see beauty in the passage of time. Nowadays, our appearance and success are constantly being evaluated against standards defined by society. *Wabi sabi* gives us the permission to stop pretending, to exist as the person who we are without disguise. In practicing the perfectly imperfect, we nurture our *kokoro* with greater dignity, compassion, and care. This is the gift *wabi sabi* offers us.

nothing lasts, nothing is perfect, nothing is complete

Nothing is eternal, yet isn't it more precious because it ends, and we still choose to love?

Nothing is flawless, yet isn't it less exhausting when we stop chasing the impossible and allow our standards to be more human?

Nothing is ever complete, yet isn't life more meaningful when it is still unfolding, and offering room to grow?

There is a simple truth in life: everything changes. It is the basic rhythm of existence. Seasons turn, bodies age, relationships evolve, and even our thoughts and perceptions transform as time passes. Our lives carry traces of time in uneven, unpredictable ways. This is not a failure of design, but a natural cycle of life.

In Japanese thought, this transience is known as *mujo*, or "impermanence". Originating in Buddhist philosophy, *mujo* is one of the Three Marks of Existence—alongside *ku* (suffering) and *muga* (non-self)—which describes the understanding that all things arise, change, and eventually pass away. Over centuries, this awareness has deeply influenced Japanese literature, art, and everyday aesthetics. Living in close relationship with nature—falling blossoms, shifting seasons, and sudden natural upheavals—has reinforced the understanding that nothing can be held permanently. Impermanence is not viewed as something to resist, but something to move with.

This sensitivity to change is felt as a soft tenderness in the heart. When we recognize that a moment will not last, we are often moved more deeply by it. In Japan, *sakura* (cherry blossoms) are cherished because they bloom brilliantly and vanish quickly. Each spring, people gather beneath the blossoms for *hanami* (flower viewing) as a ritual to enjoy the transient beauty of these delicate pink flowers. This seasonal celebration reflects *mono no aware*—the empathy and appreciation that arise when we allow ourselves to feel the beauty of something fleeting.

Through this lens, imperfection and incompleteness are not shortcomings. They are signs of life in motion. Once we accept that nothing lasts and nothing is complete, our idea of beauty also begins to change.

the impermanence of home

One place, in particular, taught me how impermanence can live quietly inside the heart.

I lived in the same house in Toronto, Canada, for more than a decade, through my teenage years, university days, and those first uncertain steps into work life. I remember the tulips rising from the soil every spring, the shrubs growing taller year by year, the winter wonderland outside the window after a snowstorm, the ache in my shoulders from shoveling the driveway. The house held me as I grew to become an adult.

Whenever I return to Toronto, I always find my way back to that street. The house belongs to someone else now; I can only stand quietly on the sidewalk and observe from the outside, careful not to disturb. I scan for what

has stayed the same—the carved wooden front door, the color of the garage doors, the big bay window facing the lawn; and what has changed—a new basketball net, a few trees gone, flowers I never planted. Each visit brings a soft tenderness in my *kokoro*—a feeling that is part gratitude, part longing. I can't go inside anymore, but fond memories flood in. Standing there, I feel *mono no aware* touch me—the bittersweet realization that those "good old days" were always passing even as I was living them, and that their very fragility is what now fills my *kokoro* with tender appreciation.

My old home taught me *wabi sabi*—how beauty deepens as life moves on—long before I had words for it.

what is beauty, really?

I once read an interview with Kyoto calligraphy artist Mikiko Kayama, whose words captured the essence of beauty more than any definition could.

When asked, "What does beauty mean to you?" Kayama said, "I think it is to be human. There is beauty to be found in imperfection. A jagged line, a broken edge, these flaws should not be disregarded. I strive to transform these unique characteristics into something beautiful and guide others to recognize their charm. It is a humble cycle to breathe life and value into the imperfect."

Our sense of beauty shapes how we live and how we treat ourselves. As humans, we naturally respond to what we find visually appealing, to things that are smooth, balanced, or impressive. Yet many of us learn to treat beauty not as an experience, but as a goal to be achieved.

Wabi sabi offers a wider, more generous way of seeing beauty. Through this lens, it is not something to acquire, maintain or perfect, but an experience that arises through attention. Here, we look into a few areas where imperfect beauty meets daily life and personal care most directly.

the living body

What if imperfections were not something to fix?

What if aging were not something to hide?

What pressure does chasing flawlessness place on our bodies and nervous system?

In contemporary culture, beauty is something we feel compelled to maintain, placing a persistent pressure on how we carry ourselves each day.

From a young age, we absorb a narrow definition of beauty through images and stories from media, culture, and social norms. Carefully curated faces, bodies, and lives become benchmarks, while anything that doesn't fit this shared template

becomes a project to fix, or a weakness to hide. We grow frustrated by gaining a few pounds, a few more lines, or simply growing older.

Many industries are built around the promise that beauty can be purchased, preserved, or perfected. Enormous amounts of time, energy, and money may be spent attempting to soften the visible traces of a lived life, instead of allowing the appearance of the natural consequences of being alive.

When we view our bodies through a lens of comparison and correction, our attention is drawn toward what is lacking without noticing our own natural beauty, which is already present.

Over time, this constant evaluation tends to generate more anxiety than confidence, more insecurity than ease. Growing older, in particular, is often framed as something to resist or conceal, even though it is a natural and inevitable part of life. The body is treated less as a living, changing presence and more as a surface that must remain controlled.

This is not to say that the desire to look nice is discouraged. Caring for our appearance can be a source of joy and a form of self-respect. The everyday choices we make reflect how we wish to present ourselves. To dress well and to groom ourselves lifts our spirits and helps us step into the world with more confidence. Beauty is not only an inward state—at every stage of life, we want to feel seen and comfortable in our own skin.

The tension begins when appearance stops being an expression of who we are and becomes a mask we wear to hide from ourselves. When the pursuit of beauty becomes a refusal of time, when it turns into erasing all signs of age and individuality rather than growing into who we are, it pulls us away from our own nature. The body is no longer lived in, as we push ourselves to meet the standards that were not designed for real human life.

the inner being

Why is it often easier to notice what is missing in us than what we already carry?

Why are we so quick to criticize ourselves, and just as quick to judge others?

What if our flaws were not failures, but expressions of individuality?

The way beauty is defined in society extends beyond appearance. Many of us are deeply conditioned from an early age by our upbringing, culture, education, and social expectations to believe we must perform well, behave properly, or display certain accomplishments. At first, these evaluations may seem like guidance to help us improve, but as they begin to sink in, they turn into a habit of self-criticism. In a perfectionist culture, when parts of us fail to meet these external ideals, we start to treat them as inner flaws to fix, hide, or eliminate.

This inner measuring stick feeds negative self-talk, built on the belief that criticism leads to growth or protection. We tell ourselves that by closely examining our perceived "shortcomings," we can stay motivated and avoid failure or rejection. Perfection is mistaken for security, and appreciation is replaced by pressure.

The same critical lens can also be projected onto others, when we rely on personal standards and expectations to judge others. We make assumptions about what they should be like, how they should respond, what they should do. When difference is not seen as individuality, we attempt to correct or reshape one another. When the inner world is lived under constant review, it becomes harder to notice beauty inside us and others.

the ordinary life

What if an unfinished life is not a failed one?

When did life become something to measure instead of experience?

What happens when our lives unfold differently from the script we were given?

Besides appearance and inner worth, we live in a culture that glorifies a specific image of what a "good" life should look like—one with a checklist to fulfill as a promise of a secure future: the right education, a successful career, a stable family, financial security. When these milestones are reached in the expected order, life is considered complete. When they are delayed, altered, or missing, it can easily be interpreted as personal failure.

This belief leaves little room for life to unfold in its own way. We learn to steer our lives toward wealth to accumulate and predefined targets to achieve. Ordinary days without visible accomplishments are dismissed as unproductive, even though they are often where life is actually happening.

Ordinary life is made up of quiet mornings, regular tasks, casual conversations, dinners eaten just like other evenings. It is lived in the in-between moments—preparing meals, waiting, tending, continuing—rather

than in visible milestones or achievements. An ordinary life is also marked by interruptions—stalled careers, shifting relationships, plans that don't work out, and periods of uncertainty, loss, or fatigue.

These are not shortcomings or setbacks, but in fact integral parts of living. Yet our attention tends to shift toward constant assessment and self-monitoring, and away from simply living our days with genuine experience. Consequently, we feel inadequate when we do not resemble the socially approved image of success. The pressure to live this image of the "good" life is exhausting, and it distances us from the realities of being human.

restoring our vision with a *wabi sabi* lens

If beauty is not something to achieve, but something to notice,

if it is not found in perfection, but in what is real,

then wabi sabi invites a different question.

Instead of asking, "How can this be made more beautiful?"

it asks, "What is already beautiful here, if I pay more attention?"

This question subtly shifts the direction of our vision. Beauty is no longer something to chase, but something that reveals itself through honesty, acceptance, and presence. It is no longer about where beauty exists, but why we so often fail to see it.

Wabi sabi invites us to see our bodies as evolving landscapes shaped by the experiences of our lives. What may be interpreted as flaws can be gateways into a fuller, more grounded beauty. It sees beauty in allowing time to leave honest marks that carry the rich interior landscape. This is what *wabi sabi* calls beautiful—the presence of a true living body.

Turning inward to our inner being, each of us carries a unique constellation of talents, traits, and perspectives. These are gifts from life itself, not achievements we earn, but qualities we are entrusted with that are waiting to be discovered and refined. When we lose sight of these gifts, we easily get into the habit of constant inner criticism. With a *wabi sabi* lens, we restore our vision to turn our attention back to what has been freely given, and learn to accept imperfections within ourselves and others.

Beauty, in this sense, emerges naturally when we live in alignment with our inner gifts. We no longer need to compare with others or criticize our imperfections. Honoring and nurturing what is uniquely ours opens the door to a more genuine way of living, where individuality can be revealed, and inner beauty can radiate through awareness, compassion, and a willingness to see what is already present.

An ordinary life also looks different when seen through this lens. Just as beauty and inner worth cannot be standardized, neither can a life—each one is marked by its own timing, individuality, and direction. Life itself has ups and downs, it's never meant to be smooth, consistent, and perfect—it is a work in progress journey, constantly changing and unfolding. Letting life unfold does not mean abandoning effort or responsibility, but loosening our attachment to rigid standards so we can meet life as it moves, rather than forcing it to conform.

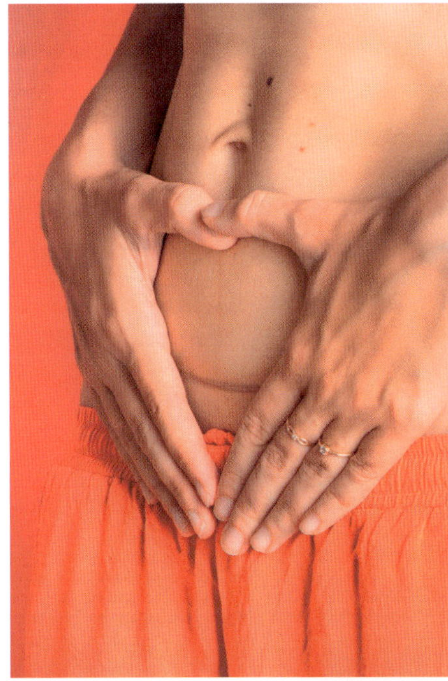

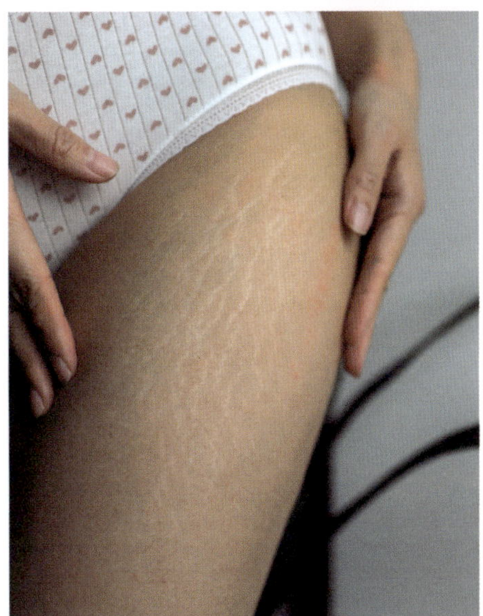

gilding imperfection in *kintsugi*

The Japanese art of *kintsugi*, introduced in the chapter on *chadō* (p. 73), offers a powerful image for restoring one's vision of beauty. In *kintsugi*, damaged objects are mended with lacquer then dusted with gold or silver powder. Cracks are left visible to become part of the object itself, symbolizing that brokenness can open new opportunities for renewal and can possibly transform into an even more beautiful version. This centuries-old art reflects a deep acceptance of impermanence: change is natural and beautiful, and imperfections in life carry depth, memory, and resilience.

"The process can help with restoring our own broken parts, both psychological and physiological. And I feel like through this job, I am also restoring the broken parts of myself," says Hiroki Kiyokawa, a Kyoto-based *kintsugi* artist.

When we restore our vision through a *wabi sabi* lens, we begin to notice beauty in our perfectly imperfect selves, and to live with greater presence. If beauty is understood as the natural uniqueness of our being, then self-care is the practice of supporting that uniqueness, and nurturing *kokoro* so our true radiance can emerge. When we stop asking whether our lives measure up, we begin to see the beauty of a life lived honestly, one day at a time.

wabi sabi self-reflection self-care ritual

Practicing *wabi sabi* principles can be a gentle and nourishing form of self-care. Set aside time regularly—perhaps weekly, monthly, or quarterly—to sit with the reflections below. Approach them not through the lens of perfection, but with openness, patience, and kindness.

You may wish to choose a journal that feels meaningful to you and return to these questions whenever you feel the need to reconnect with yourself. There is no right or wrong

way to respond, and no need to answer everything at once. Let your reflections unfold naturally, just as life does.

As time passes, revisiting these questions may reveal how your understanding, values, and sense of self have shifted. Rather than seeking resolution, this practice may help liberate you from self-criticism, loosen judgment, and create space for acceptance. Let *wabi sabi* be a guiding light, inspiring you to move toward a life that feels honest, grounded, and beautiful enough as it is.

◆ Perfection and self-expectation:
In what areas of your life do you feel pressure to be perfect?

How do you usually respond when things do not go according to plan?

How do you feel when you allow room for mistakes or uncertainty?

◆ Seeing yourself with kindness:
How would a close friend describe your strengths and qualities?

What parts of yourself do you tend to judge most harshly?

What might change if you met these parts with compassion instead of criticism?

◆ Imperfection as individuality:
In what ways might your "imperfections" shape your perspective and choices, and how might they allow you to appreciate yourself with more warmth and respect?

Can you recall a moment in your life that reflects the spirit of wabi sabi*—something unfinished, imperfect, or unexpected that later showed its value?*

Are you willing to accept differences in your partner, friends, and family, and to respect their irregularities as unique qualities?

◆ An ordinary, unfinished life:
What does a "perfect life" mean to you? Where did this idea come from?

How does this image differ from a life that feels honest or meaningful?

Are there areas of your life that feel unfinished or unresolved, and what might it be like to allow them to remain so, for now?

◆ Time, change, and acceptance:
How do you relate to the passage of time, both in your body and in your life story?

Are there past experiences, changes, or versions of yourself that you are still resisting?

What might it feel like to make peace with what time has shaped, rather than trying to erase it?

生き甲斐

ikigai (reason for being)

Purpose is often described as a guiding compass in life, which helps us make choices about how we live. We associate it with meaningful engagement, and with using our strengths and skills in ways that contribute value beyond ourselves. A sense of purpose can fill our days with motivation, reassurance, and a sense of significance. But when this purpose feels unclear or life shifts in ways that disrupts it, we may feel lost or uncertain, as though we have failed to become who we were meant to be.

a reason to get up in the morning

As morning light seeps through the curtains, the alarm rings, and we get out of bed to meet the responsibilities of the day. We keep moving, following what we believe we should do, often without questioning why and rarely stopping to ask what makes any of it feel worthwhile.

Having lived in a bustling city for most of my life, I often find myself watching people drifting through the streets with an empty, unfocused gaze, as if their bodies are on autopilot while their minds are elsewhere, pulled far away from their physical reality. Their faces look drawn and weary. Shoulders are stiff and hunched, carrying what appears to be years of accumulated tension. There is little sign of vitality and vibrancy, only exhaustion, disconnection, and a heaviness that comes from the relentless pace and

demands of daily life, which allow little time to truly breathe.

In my coaching work, I have come to see that many of these people are not failing at life: I often listen to people who are capable, committed, doing what they are "supposed" to do, and many of them are even labeled "successful," yet something essential seems to be missing. They have dedicated years of effort and care to a role or responsibility, only to feel lost when that role changes, ends, or no longer provides a sense of meaning. Life has become a list of obligations rather than something they feel genuinely connected to. Each morning begins not with joy, but the weight of another day to get through.

Often, this happens when meaning has slowly narrowed. One role—whether work, caregiving, or another responsibility—becomes the primary, or sometimes the only, source of identity, structure, and self-worth. Other parts of life fall out of focus: rest, hobbies, play, supportive relationships. When life relies on a single pillar, it can feel stable for a long time, but when that pillar cracks—from burnout, disappointment, redundancy, change in circumstances, or simply a fading sense of being alive—the entire structure is shaken, and we begin to wonder, "What am I really here for?"

As we come to the last chapter of this book, there is no expectation to uncover one grand life purpose. Rather, it is an invitation to reflect on what makes getting up each morning feel worthwhile, even on days that feel uncertain or difficult. Here, it offers a different way of relating to meaning, one that emerges gradually through ordinary life, unforced, incomplete, and deeply personal.

This is *ikigai*.

ikigai simply lived

You may have encountered *ikigai* described in a similar way: as a framework for finding purpose at the intersection of what you love, what you're good at, what the world needs, and what brings income. While this interpretation can be useful, it reflects a modern, Western-influenced lens—one that emphasizes optimization, alignment, clarity, and financial return, particularly in relation to work and career.

Here, I return to how *ikigai* is more commonly lived and understood in everyday Japanese life.

In Japanese, *iki* means "life" and *gai* means "value" or "worth." Put together, *ikigai* is often understood as "what makes life worthwhile" or "a reason for being." It is less a concrete identity or goal to reach, and more a felt sense of what makes life worthwhile. It can be a person, an activity, a place, a role—

anything that brings aliveness and meaning into daily life.

Ikigai is not necessarily about career, status, or achievement, but is found in small joys, familiar routines, relationships, community bonds, and a sense of contribution. It may be caring for a family member, cooking for loved ones, practicing a craft, supporting the community, or finding simple pleasure in everyday moments. These reasons do not need to be impressive, profitable, or permanent, they simply offer a reason to get up in the morning.

Ikigai is not a single life mission, nor something to identify once and hold forever. It can shift across different stages of life, and we may have several *ikigai* at the same time, each connected to different aspects of life. When we release the pressure to define a final purpose, life can still feel worth living even when it is imperfect, incomplete, or demanding, as long as there are reasons, however small, that keep us connected to it.

One of the most beautiful descriptions of *ikigai* I've heard came not from a book, but from a Japanese friend, Shoko Yaginuma, a forester and retreat leader living in Minakami of Gunma Prefecture.

"My ikigai *is to listen deeply to the voices of local people and nature, and to gently support those voices as they find expression in harmony with the wider world. Caring for the forest and creating retreats with local people are both part of this. I find deep meaning in listening to what the trees want to become, and to the pain and hopes of the community, and helping carry them into the future."* **Shoko Yaginuma**

This description is modest, yet deeply meaningful. It is grounded in everyday attention, relationships, and care—something that grows through listening, participation, and time.

Ikigai is not a new idea introduced at the end of this book. It is the place where everything we have explored so far naturally comes together in daily life.

how meaning and happiness grow over time

When people hear the words "meaning" and "happiness," they often fall back on specific associations. "Happiness" is usually associated with positive emotions of joy, contentment, and pleasure. "Meaning," on the other hand, is generally understood as having a clear purpose, and a sense that everything adds up to something worthwhile. Together, the two words can sound like a promise of a good life that is both deeply purposeful and consistently positive.

Because of this expectation, meaning and happiness can carry hope, but also pressure, as if we are expected to feel good and have our direction already figured out. A common misunderstanding is the assumption that we must first clearly identify and justify our meaning, and that happiness will follow. When a satisfying "why" does not appear on demand, life can start to feel like personal failure, rather than a normal, changing human experience.

In listening to people over the years, I often hear a familiar story. After long periods of hard work, people realize they no longer enjoy what they do. They feel exhausted, disconnected, and dissatisfied with their jobs, yet struggle to see a realistic alternative. So much time and energy have been invested in building their current lives that starting over feels impossible. Income is still needed. Responsibilities remain. And life continues as it is—an endless loop of dissatisfaction, obligation, and fatigue, where meaning and joy gradually fade.

At this point, many people assume the answer lies in finding a clearer purpose or a different direction. But what if, instead of waiting for a defining

calling, we first learn how to restore meaning and quiet joy in ordinary life? This is where *ikigai*, as it is lived in everyday Japanese life, offers a more realistic and sustainable starting point.

Restoration often begins with paying attention to small moments of joy. Not joy as excitement or achievement, but signs that life still feels inhabitable: the pleasure of a morning walk, time spent noticing the change of season, a conversation with a friend that feels inspiring. These moments may seem insignificant, yet they matter. They show that *kokoro*, the heart-mind, is still responding—softening, easing, awakening, turning back toward life.

Drawing on both Japanese perspectives and modern insights from coaching and well-being work, I've noticed that meaning and happiness tend to grow through three overlapping movements: grounding, widening, and orientation. These are not a sequence to follow, but recurring conditions in which *ikigai* fades and returns.

Grounding allows *kokoro* to settle.

Widening gives *kokoro* something to respond to.

Orientation emerges when we trust what *kokoro* has been showing us.

Grounding restores stability. When someone is chronically stressed, exhausted, or overwhelmed, the body stays on alert, and the mind narrows. Even meaningful opportunities can feel like burdens. Grounding re-establishes a secure sense of self, emotional balance, and presence. This is where self-care matters—getting enough rest, tending to the body, and managing stress so the nervous system can stabilize. When grounding is absent, happiness is often confused with brief relief, and meaning remains difficult to access.

Widening creates space. As grounding returns, life begins to open. There is room to rediscover interests, relationships, and small pleasures. Ordinary moments begin to reappear: reconnecting with friends, picking up a new hobby, making space to simply be with yourself. Time is created that is not organized entirely around obligation. When you are absorbed in activities you enjoy, a heartfelt sense of satisfaction and well-being can arise. As life widens, meaning is no longer defined by a single role or responsibility. Happiness at this stage often appears as curiosity and a renewed sense of engagement with life.

Orientation emerges. Not a fixed plan or final answer, orientation rarely arrives as a sudden revelation. It often shows up as a gentle sense of direction—a quiet pull from the heart toward ways of contributing, creating, or being useful that feel aligned with who a person is becoming. Many people are surprised to discover that clarity comes after life feels more stable and spacious, not before. Bigger life choices that once felt impossible to make begin to take shape through lived experience.

Rather than asking, "What is my purpose?", the question now becomes, "Is the way I'm living making room for meaning and joy to grow?" This shift reduces pressure. We can remain where we are, even in imperfect or constrained situations, while taking small steps to restore joy and connection. This way *ikigai* is lived: not as an escape from life, but as a way of living more fully, one ordinary day at a time.

practicing *ikigai* as a daily relationship

To practice *ikigai* as a daily relationship means to let meaning be ordinary. *Ikigai* is not something we find once, but something we relate to in the course of time. When we treat *ikigai* in this way, self-care stops being a project of self-improvement and becomes a trusted companion.

Practicing *ikigai* begins with listening to *kokoro*. We allow *kokoro* to settle first, then respond when given space. We don't need to constantly ask ourselves whether we are "on the right track." Instead of demanding answers, we focus on cultivating the right conditions. We stay in relationship with our inner compass and with everyday life.

The following self-care practice supports grounding, widening, and orientation, so meaning can emerge naturally.

ikigai self-care practice: arriving through grounding, widening, and orientation

This practice helps you feel present, spacious, and oriented before engaging with meaning. It can be done once a day, or at anytime you feel rushed, disconnected, or unclear. Find a quiet corner, prepare a notebook or journal, a pen, and a warm drink.

1. Grounding (arriving in your life)

◆ Stand or sit comfortably with both feet firmly on the floor, let your hands rest naturally at the sides or in your lap.

◆ Notice the weight of your body, the support beneath you, the rhythm of your breath.

◆ Silently acknowledge: "I am here."

◆ Take a few breaths. On each exhale, feel your weight settling down into the chair, the floor, the ground.

◆ If your mind is busy, anchor your attention on one simple sensation: the warmth of your hands, the feeling of your feet, or the rise and fall of your breath.

2. Widening (making space for what nourishes)

◆ Let awareness gently expand outward.

◆ Notice the space around you, sounds near and far, the feeling of air on your skin. Let attention widen naturally.

◆ Silently acknowledge:
"There is room."

◆ Write down three small things that felt nourishing recently.

Examples: the taste of miso soup, laughing with my colleague, the warmth of winter sun.

◆ Pick one of them and ask: "How could I give myself a little more of this today or this week?"

Examples:
"Today I will take my afternoon tea away from my desk."
"Tonight I will walk once around the block after dinner."

3. Orientation (listening for direction)

◆ Place your hand on your chest or belly and close your eyes for a moment.

◆ Silently acknowledge: "I am in relationship with my life."

◆ Ask: "What feels most important to care for right now?"

Examples: a relationship, your health, a hobby, rest, learning, or simple stability.

◆ Let a sense, word, or feeling arise, even if it seems small or obvious.

◆ If it doesn't arise today, that is perfectly fine. No need to search for an answer.

◆ Write that word or phrase too:
"Today I am caring for: __."

◆ Add the one small thing from the widening step above.

Examples:
"Taking tea away from my desk helps me care for my health and focus."
"Walking after dinner helps me care for my mood and sleep."

This links your small act of self-care with a direction that matters to you, so it is not just "another habit" but part of your living *ikigai.*

4. Closing the Ritual

Thank yourself for taking the time for practicing: "Thank you for caring for what matters to me."

a letter to you

Thank you for walking with me through these pages.

As you read, you may have recognized pieces of your own days. Perhaps the warmth of a bath at the end of a long week, a simple meal you prepared, a walk under trees, a cup of tea held with two hands, a few breaths of stillness before sleep. Perhaps something in you softened when we spoke of letting go, or when we lingered with the beauty of imperfect, changing things. These moments belong to you now. They are no longer just ideas from Japan, they have become part of your everyday life.

Self-care, as explored throughout this book, is not only about recovering from stress or managing exhaustion, or finding momentary relief without attending to deeper needs. It is how we protect the inner conditions that allow our true self to emerge. When life becomes crowded or demanding, what we lose first is not purpose, but the capacity to notice what matters and return to it.

Ikigai holds self-care together. It turns scattered tools into a single practice and a living relationship. In this way, self-care becomes less about fixing yourself and more about staying in conversation with your life—a relationship that grows and changes as you do.

Start where you are. Care for what keeps you connected. Let meaning build through consistent participation rather than pressure, with a little more attention, a little more kindness, a little more willingness to notice what matters to you. And when things shift, as they always do, you will no longer be relying on just one source of meaning.

This book is not meant to push you forward or provide a solid answer. It's here to offer room to rest, room to notice, room to reconnect with what brings joy and makes getting up in the morning feel meaningful. Let the practices be small anchors, a way of saying to yourself, "My well-being matters, even on ordinary days." Keep them beside you as life unfolds in its own rhythm, guiding you to meet your days as a human being—imperfect, changing, and still deeply worth living.

May you keep finding small, joyful reasons to be here.

With Love,
Iris

resources

BOOKS

Your Guide to Forest Bathing: Experience the Healing Power of Nature, by M. Amos Clifford (Red Wheel, 2021)

The Japanese Teahouse, by Wolfgang Fehrer (Niggli, 2019)

The Book of Ichigo Ichie: The Art of Making the Most of Every Moment, the Japanese Way, by Héctor García and Francesc Miralles (Penguin Books, 2019)

Ikigai: The Japanese Secret to a Long and Happy Life, by Héctor García and Francesc Miralles (Hutchinson London, 2017)

Kokoro: Japanese Wisdom for a Life Well Lived, by Beth Kempton (Storey Publishing, LLC, 2014)

Wabi Sabi: Japanese Wisdom for a Perfectly Imperfect Life, by Beth Kempton (Piatkus, 2018)

The Onsen Experience: A Guide to Japan's Hot Spring Sanctuaries, by Iris Law (Man Mo Media, 2020)

The Japanese Art of Living Seasonally, by Natalie Leon (Watkins, 2024)

Shinrin-Yoku: The Art and Science of Forest-Bathing, by Dr. Qing Li (Penguin Life, 2018)

How to Let Things Go, by Shunmyō Masuno (Penguin Life, 2024)

Zen: The Art of Simple Living, by Shunmyō Masuno (Michael Joseph, 2019)

Awakening Your Ikigai: How the Japanese Wake Up to Joy and Purpose Every Day, by Ken Mogi (The Experiment, 2018)

Becoming Yourself: Teachings on the Zen Way of Life, by Shunryū Suzuki (Particular Books, 2025)

Zen Mind, Beginner's Mind, by Shunryū Suzuki (Shambhala, 2011)

The Essence of Shinto: Japan's Spiritual Heart, by Motohisa Yamakage (Kodansha International, 2012)

Ikigai: The Japanese Secret to a Long and Happy Life, by Francesc Miralles and Hector Garcia (Hutchinson London, 2017)

OTHER RESOURCES

"Zazen as a Way of Harmonizing the Self: Dharma Talk," by Rev. Issho Fujita (Upaya Zen Center) <www.youtube.com/watch?v=G7R3IDKokNs>

"Ultra-processed food exposure and adverse health outcomes: umbrella review of epidemiological meta-analyses," by Melissa M Lane et al. (*British Medical Journal* 384:e077310 (2024)) <doi.org/10.1136/bmj-2023-077310>

"'Temizuya': The Cleansing Ritual," by Toya Manabu <www.nippon.com/en/views/b05205>

Musubi Academy <www.musubi.academy/articles/>

"Educational philosophies of self-cultivation: Chinese humanism," by Michael A. Peters (*Educational Philosophy and Theory* 54 (2022): 1720–1726) <doi.org/10.1080/00131857.2020.1811679>

"Profile: Lacquer Art Restorer Hiroki Suezaki" <heiando-kyoto.com/profile/>

'Religion and Healing in Pre-Modern Japan', by Pamela D. Winfield (*Religion Compass* 6/11 (2012): 467–479) <doi.org/10.1111/rec3.12020>

index

PICTURE CREDITS

All photos © Adobe Stock unless otherwise indicated.

Cover Billal, Andrei, norikko; **1 border** Samolevsky; **1 picture** Andrei; **3** Rajbala, Creative Image; **4** daniela; **5** Jan Baldwin © Ryland Peters & Small; **6** norikko; **8** leungchopan; **9** Amit World; **10** barks; **11** anujakjaimook; **12–13** navintar; **14** vikusha_art; **15** swasdee; **16** Thanapong; **17** above shosa; **17** below © Iris Law; **18** Madrugada Verde; **19** Interior Design; **20** above Eric Akashi; **20** below Andrei; **21** above left Tomo; **21** above right wooooooojpn; **21** below shiryu01; **22** above left sahachat; **22** above right aaron90311; **22** below Andrea Aigner; **23** Julia Laime; **24** Nelli Valova; **25** above left Viktor; **25** above right Kotkoa; **25** below Home-stock; **26** Yuki Sugiura © Ryland Peters & Small; **27** Andrei; **28–29** Yuki Sugiura © Ryland Peters & Small **30** Ed Andersen © Ryland Peters & Small; **31** Yuki Sugiura © Ryland Peters & Small; **32** buritora; **33** Yuki Sugiura © Ryland Peters & Small; **34** Yuki Sugiura © Ryland Peters & Small; **34** border daniela; **35** Yuki Sugiura © Ryland Peters & Small; **37** SeanPavonePhoto; **38** Samolevsky; **39** left ibuki; **39** middle Askanioff; **39** right Askanioff; **40** left norikko; **40** right TM; **42** Leckerstudio; **43** MDMOHOBBAT; **45** Elsie; **46–47** © Iris Law **48** TheWaterMeloonProjec; **50** Drazen; **51** Kitinut; **54** Ed; **55** left and right © Iris Law; **56** west_photo; **57** above left Pongvit; **57** above right KaWataru; **57** below T i M e L a P s E; **58** left Africa Studio; **58** right Limages Studio; **59** Catherine Gratwicke © Ryland Peters & Small; **60** above & below Ed; **62** Jan Baldwin © Ryland Peters & Small; **63** Aleksei_7799; **64–65** serena; **67** above torsakarin; **67** below mex99; **68** left oneinchpunch; **68** right Jan Baldwin © Ryland Peters & Small **69** norikko; **70** Jan Baldwin © Ryland Peters & Small; **71** Florent; **72** Federico Magonio; **74** riyat; **75** above svetlanakononov7; **75** below Lin; **77** Pixel-Shot; **79** New Africa; **80–81** 温子 河口; **83** sand555; **85** pressmaster; **88** above 4315; **88** below left Lily; **88** below right Zoey 106; **91** Ken Tyler; **91** border marylia17; **92** anatoliil; **94** Sammi's World; **95** login2002; **96–97** Klodien; **98** Cristina Conti; **99** Tonic Ray Sonic; **100** Oleksandr; **101** RaptorWoman; **102** above left, center, right Dan Duchars/CONTENTed Nest © Ryland Peters & Small; **102** below sunti; **103** Benjamin Edwards © Ryland Peters & Small; **104** Prostock-studio; **105** above Marco Montalti; **105** below Pinkasevich; **109** above 22August; **109** below left Rubberhorse; **109** below right Chrstine Bird; **110–111** kasa; **113** Emily_M_Wilson; **115** Paula; **116** above eggeeggjiew; **116** below N F/peopleimages.com; **119** Nadiya Nacorda; **121** above troyanphoto; **121** below Mykola; **122** bondarillia **125** Farknot Architect; **126–127** yanikap; **129** Hockley Media/peopleimages.com; **130** Lukas Gojda; **131** Paul Rushton; **132** above left Alex; **132** above center © Iris Law; **132** above right Oksana; **132** below Andreja Donko; **133** mimagephotos; **134** Smile; **135** fizkes; **139** © Iris Law

acknowledgments

Dad, my role model of resilience, integrity, righteousness, diligence, and humility—without these values, I would not have had the vision to write this book. Mom, for being the first to care for my health, and for encouraging me to help others care for theirs. My sister Heidie, forever my little sister and ally through life's ups and downs. Once again, you took care of me while I disappeared into my writing world.

CICO Books—Carmel, Julia, Imogen, Toni, and Emily—for trusting me to write this book and for giving me the opportunity to share my love and respect for Japan, as well as my passion for health and wellness. It's such a joy working with you on this book.

Theresa, Sharon, your professional and thoughtful advice made this book possible.

Friends who traveled with me to Japan, for being part of the journey. These pages carry memories we shared together. You know who you are.

The people in Japan whose paths I was fortunate to cross: you were living examples of Japanese values. The lessons you shared and the lives you lived have left a lasting imprint on me. This book is, in many ways, a reflection of the wisdom I received from you.

Gallant, for standing by me wherever I go and whatever I do. I couldn't have written this book without the incredible journeys we shared exploring Japan and the world together—my partner and soulmate, then, now and always.

Above all, praise to You, Almighty God, for revealing Your presence through the beauty of nature. Moments in nature have enlightened me to love and honor Your creation as a mirror of Your grace.